THOTH

The L... Atlantis

An interpretation by
Malcolm S. Southwood

Copyright © Malcolm S. Southwood 2021
This book is sold subject to the condition that it shall not, by way of trade or otherwise, be lent, resold, hired out, or otherwise circulated without the publisher's prior consent in any form of binding or cover other than that in which it is published and without a similar condition including this condition being imposed on the subsequent publisher.
The moral right of Malcolm S. Southwood has been asserted.
ISBN-13: 9798513409069

*This work is dedicated to the Higher Beings
of our universe,
who never tire from showing us the Path of Salvation.*

*Also a special thanks to all the souls involved in
maintaining, conveying and translating
the ancient wisdom.*

Malcolm Southwood is an acclaimed international healer, public speaker, author and teacher. He has spent the bigger part of his life helping people with their health and inner contentment, answering questions of practical as well as other worldly aspects at lectures and workshops around the world.

Many of his teachings and healing techniques are inspired by his observation of nature, which he acquired during the early part of his life while working in agriculture and establishing a close connection to the natural world and its *forces*. Born in 1940, it was only in

1982 that he discovered his healing abilities and began a new journey in life, helping over 30,000 people with their physical and emotional problems along the way.

Owing to his success, he has also been invited to give lectures and workshops to medical personnel in major health institutions such as the Basel Psychiatric Hospital in Switzerland and the Thomas Jefferson University Hospital in Philadelphia. The World Presidents Association (WPO) has also shown interest in his methods and invited him to speak at their annual conference on three different occasions.

To help raise awareness and understanding about health and well-being, and the spiritual part of life, he has already published several books. Including:

You And Your Mobile Home
Where The Soul Flies
Pyramids Of The Mind
Teach Me How To Love
The Healing Experience
A Helping Hand With Children

CONTENTS

PREFACE i
INTRODUCTION 1
BEFORE THE FLOOD 6
   The Flood 14
AFTER THE FLOOD 18
   Emotion in Place 26
PYRAMIDS OF ATLANTIS 32
LORD LIFE AND DEATH 40
   Light and Dark 43
   Thoth's Pathway to Light 49
WINDOWS OF THE MIND 57
   Meditation for an Out-of-Body Experience 62
   Prayer for Ascension 63
THE LOST PLANE OF ATLANTIS 65
   The Astral World 71
   Sphinx and Pyramid 75
ASCENSION 78
   The Seven Masters 86
   In the Light 92
MYSTERIES 100
THE WORD 115
SPIRALS 126
   Circles within Circles 131
THE DOCTRINE 141
THE BEGINNING 148

PREFACE

Dear Reader,

The first time that I heard of the Emerald Tablets was in 1995, when a lady walked into my office in Florida, dropped a pile of loosely bound papers onto my desk and said, 'I think these are meant for you...'

She then turned around, walked out, and I never saw her again.

At the time I didn't take too much notice of the papers, except to notice the title on the front cover – *"The Emerald Tablets of Thoth the Atlantean"*.

Since then, I have travelled extensively across America, Germany and Switzerland, carrying as little luggage as possible, but for some reason that loosely bound pile of papers followed me everywhere – like a little dog, who refuses to be left behind.

I briefly read through them from time to time, but nothing stirred me to take a serious interest in the contents until I was back in England in the spring of 2020. I was wondering what to read when, from seemingly nowhere, the pile of loosely bound papers appeared on my desk again, looking at me with an appealing eye, saying, *'Read me.'*

It was then that I began to take seriously what Thoth

many thousands of years ago had recorded, verifying his life as an Atlantean before and after the famous flood.

I first read the translation, which is the work of Dr. Doreal, and then his interpretation, but the interpretation was too abstract and did not make any sense. It was as if someone was sitting on my shoulder, saying, *'Can't they understand that Atlantis is an ethereal place, in a higher dimension?'* which is how the following interpretation was written.

The whole of this writing is inspired, it was as if I had been lifted into another world that hosts an enormous library of information. I therefore take no credit for what you are about to read, except maybe in the style of writing.

I hope you enjoy your travels with Thoth as much as I did, and because of them come to understand yourself and your destiny more fully than before you began this journey.

Malcolm S. Southwood

There is one thing stronger than all the armies in the world, and that is an idea whose time has come.
- Victor Hugo -

INTRODUCTION

THOTH BEGAN HIS LIFE in a great city on an island, which was one of the planes of the Continent of Atlantis. Atlantis was constructed on ten different levels, each one of which was in its own spiritually separate space to the ones above or below. Atlantis should not be thought of as something earthly, but as something ethereal, and though the Masters could descend to the planes below, the people who lived on the lower planes were unable to raise their awareness high enough to move to a higher plane.

Thoth didn't live his life like people today, who live in streets of houses, go to work or school, drive around in cars, shop in the local supermarket, pay taxes, have bank accounts and spend most of their time stressed about what might happen or hasn't happened.

Like most people of that time, Thoth's life was one of leisurely luxury, even though they lived on the lowest of the ten planes, or islands. There was an abundance of food. Their need for food was far less than what we would consider necessary today and what they did eat was uncooked, mostly exotic fruit and vegetables, and no one ever thought of eating meat.

There was no system of money exchange and most goods and services were bartered. Neither was there any thought of private ownership, except for the responsibility they felt towards the homes they lived in. There were no factories, offices, or other means of employment. Household appliances such as washing machines, fridges, vacuum cleaners etc. did not exist, there was simply no need for them.

The air was pure and clean, the atmosphere fresh and untainted, and any little washing that was necessary was done in local rivers or streams. There were no hospitals, though there were people in the community who had studied the value of plants and relied on herbs and other plant-based medicines when it was necessary, which was not often.

It was an idyllic life, free of stress and fear. Children played in the fields and streams and any schooling was done in unorganised groups. The teachers were people who had an interest in children's needs and cared for their interests out of affection, rather than any need for reward or authority.

On the plane of Atlantis where Thoth grew up, people lived for over two hundred years. They did not age as we know it today. They were careful to ensure that the energies of the body were always kept in balance. They understood that health was dependent on fresh food, fresh water and a stress-free life, and anything that added to the stresses of life was to be avoided.

When they began to feel tired and their life-energies draining away, they would lie down in the quiet of their noise-free homes and, using a hypnotic meditation, sing themselves into a final sleep. They knew they would wake up in a higher realm than the one they were leaving, and they would arrive in a place where they could restore their spiritual energies, their life-force. If they had prepared themselves for this transition with study and gathered enough experience and knowledge during their existence on the island, they would either move on to exist in a higher awareness or, after a long and restful interval, return and start afresh.

There was no feeling of loss by those who were left behind, no mourning, no prayers. Emotion as we understand it had not yet infected the World of Atlantis. Overwhelming appreciation for all life, equally and without favouritism, was the way in which the people of Atlantis saw each other. There were no tears of loss, just love for the life that would be born to replace the one who had gone. The bodies which had been vacated would simply dissolve into mist, like all other unwanted material. The air was so pure and free of destructive vibrations, such as fear, that when matter was no longer needed some force of nature took back what it had given.

Religion as we understand it was also unknown, but there were people amongst them who they recognised as masters. Men and women alike, since there is no supremacy on either side, who had studied the Laws of Creation and had strong radiant energies, were the ones chosen to guide the people in the correct ways of life and nature. A master's energy had the ability to heal, to balance the needs of growing crops and to control the wild animals that roamed freely through their world – fear of any sort was unknown.

The masters met and consulted in a temple, which was the central point of this island of Atlantis, and which was the focus for communication with the Masters of Light from the planes beyond their own. It was in quiet contemplation that the chosen masters communicated with the Lords from the higher realms. The masters who had studied the Laws of their Universe were trained to receive the thought-communicated messages from the Masters of Light, who held themselves responsible for the general welfare of all people on the Continent of Atlantis.

Thoth had lived during the times of greatness on this island of Atlantis and also through the times of its demise, when it had been separated from the main body to fall into a lower sphere, losing the support of the laws and structure that the Continent of Atlantis had provided.

During all of this time, Thoth had been reborn many times, and each time his strength had been renewed and his knowledge of the Laws of Life had increased. He had reached the heights of wisdom and was determined to leave a record of his knowledge, to help the people who were willing to follow him. He believed this to be his purpose before he could retire from the world of people. People, who also needed to progress through a series of lives to the high status of Light Beings, before they could return to the Continent of Atlantis.

Thoth left a record of his experiences and knowledge with men[1], both female and male, who were to be responsible for keeping the knowledge unaltered and in its original state as he said, *'There is only one truth.'*

During its telling and retelling over thousands of years, Thoth's wisdom and philosophy became the basis of the Egyptian belief. Thoth emphasised that the students, to whom he entrusted this great knowledge and wisdom, must be sure not to adulterate his teachings with thoughts and beliefs of their own.

He promised that one day, he would return to either reward or punish those who made themselves responsible for passing on his knowledge and wisdom, according to how they have honoured or misused their privileged position as leaders.

Thoth now wants his wisdom to be re-told in a way that it will be understood in the 21st century, as so much of it has been forgotten, changed or partially lost.

---

[1] Man (pl. men) = short-form of humanity/mankind: including both female and male gender.

BEFORE THE FLOOD

AT THE BEGINNING OF TIME, the people of Atlantis were great beyond the understanding of the people who live today. They had knowledge and wisdom that was born from the heart of the Light and all that they needed was provided for them. Life on Atlantis was bliss, with no fear of loss or need, and life existed in many different forms and expressions.

Beauty was born in the thoughts of the people who lived there and showed itself in expressions of art in all its various forms. The power and the happiness found in these lands was because of the light that flowed through all the planes of Atlantis.

These people were born strong, with the energy that came from the centre of the Light, which was set in the highest of the ten planes. Thoth's father was the most knowledgeable and wisest of all people on this island of Atlantis, and he was therefore the master to them all.

He was granted the responsibility of caring for the temple, which was built over a vortex that led to the higher planes, and it was through this vortex that the

Spirits of Light, known as the Masters of Light, could come and go as they pleased.

Thoth's father, because of the power of his mind-energy, was chosen to be the link between the Masters of Light and his people. He received instructions on the way life was to be lived through the unspoken thoughts between himself and the Great Lord (God), who dwelt on the highest of the ten worlds of this great ethereal continent called Atlantis.

On the lower planes were the lesser Children of Light. But all of this was before the great flood. Earth, which is on this lowest plane of Atlantis, became lost in its own darkness, causing it to separate from the wonders and beauty of the Great Continent and eventually become covered in water, which we know as the flood.

But Thoth grew up in a time when Earth was still part of Great Atlantis and where, under the guidance of his father, he was taught the mysteries and laws that govern the life of the people of their world. As he grew into manhood, he was consumed by a need to know more. Unlike other young people, he asked for nothing but to be given the knowledge that leads to wisdom. He spent his time talking to the masters, asking questions about the beginning of time, the wonders of space, and what they knew of the planes above their own.

During his training he learned how to talk to the Spirits of Nature, who shared with him their secrets of life in the treetops, and the world of life in the ground below the roots. He saw that in the colour of a flower was every colour imaginable, and that it is the most vibrant of all these colours that dominates the flower's appearance.

He was shown how to move with the energy of insects who, as friends of the plants, carried the wonders of nature's creation from plant to plant, and tree to tree. He was able to take his thoughts and be one with the energy and awareness of the birds and animals, as they moved from place to place, and how to be content in their contentment. He watched over them while they slept, keeping them safe and cloaked in the compassion that nature had passed on to him, as a gift for his thoughtfulness.

And when that time came for them to return home to greater awareness, he would take their precious little bodies into his hands and release their souls into the world, where he was yet to follow.

Thoth spent his young life learning laws that only nature could teach. His yearning to know more of nature's secrets and its laws, that even his teachers could not know, was so overwhelming that one day, while he was dreaming under a sleepy willow tree, he was commanded by the Great Lord of Atlantis to enter into the Temple of Light. Thoth told his father what he had been instructed to do and so his father stood him in the centre of the Light, from where Thoth was conveyed onto the highest of the ten planes of Atlantis.

He found himself standing outside a beautiful oblong temple, glittering with shades of colour he had never seen before. He was surrounded by people who were dressed in garments of white and as he started towards the temple, the people parted to let him through. He mounted the steps and entered into the Great Temple.

The structure of the building shimmered with the colours of music and as the notes changed, so did the colours. The Great Temple seemed to be alive with a quiet peace, which filled all the space within the temple walls. The air was vibrant with a soft pink glow that carried the perfume of the most delicate of roses.

Thoth felt himself floating gently through the crowd of people, who were standing with their heads bowed, until he found himself at the steps of a great golden dais. The floor beneath his feet felt as soft as any cloud he had watched sliding through the skies above his homeland in Lower Atlantis.

Seated on a golden throne was the Lord of all Lords, who radiated a powerful golden light, which was at the same time as soft and gentle as any newly born life. Then the Lord of all Lords, the Great Lord, spoke to Thoth.

'There are very few who have the level of light you show and are honoured to be lifted out of their heavy bodies to enter this Great Temple and stand before me and the light beings present here, before death has released them...

'Your yearning Thoth, for knowledge and wisdom, has brought you to the notice of the Spirits of Light who surround you, and you are to be granted your wish to be free to learn from the Masters of Light.'

The temple was filled with Spirits of Light who were dressed in white gowns, all the same youthful age and with beautiful radiant faces. It was impossible to know what gender they were, if they were male or female, since they were in such perfect balance.

These Spirits of Light were not like people he had seen on the lower planes. They had not been required to incarnate into a heavy, physical body and so they were able to move freely and without effort into any of the lower planes, where they were seen as moving lights. Lights so brilliant that mortals from Lower Atlantis would have been unable to look upon them, if they had not shaded the brightness of their being with a darker cloak.

Thoth had been chosen from amongst mortals to be taught the mysteries of creation, so that eventually he would be able to bring into being an idea that was still in its infancy at that time. There was a plan already being prepared, which would give everyone the opportunity to move onto a higher plane after earthly life had finished.

For eons, Thoth lived in the Temple of Light learning all there was to know of the wisdom that came from the great minds, the Masters of the ten planes of Atlantis.

And eventually he was brought before them, the Guardians of the Eternal Flame, as they were called.

This world was wrapped in darkness to protect the visitor from the brilliance of its light, a light so bright that it would hurt and blind anyone whose thoughts were not equal to the purity of the Flame. There, in this shaded world, sat the Masters on their thrones of infinite power, radiating light that is beyond mortal understanding.

Thoth was overwhelmed by the intensity of the welcome, and the honour he felt standing before these all-powerful Masters, who told him that he had succeeded in his task of learning, and that they were pleased to honour him with the Keys to Eternal Life[2].

He realised that he was now protected from all negative influence, and free to move through the forces that hold the different planes of Atlantis together – yet separate – as one continent. He had become free to explore the various higher planes of Atlantis, and also to journey into the Underworlds of dark emotional energy, which had become a growing threat to the balance of the whole continent. He could now journey into the dark waves of emotion, to learn what it was that held mankind to their allotted time and space, and the Cycles of Life and Death.

---

[2] Which the Egyptians would later symbolise by the Ankh ☥, meaning that the person holding the Ankh held the Keys to Eternal Life and could therefore move freely through the different planes of Atlantis.

He was now free to travel beyond the stars, and beyond the limits of time. This was his reward for searching for truth and wisdom. He was handed the keys to search in the space of the universe and learn of greater mysteries. Thoth had understood that only in the search for truth and the mysteries of life, can wisdom be found.

Down through the ages, Thoth saw others leaving their bodies only to be reborn again, and again, always back into the same lower dimension from which they had come. He watched waves of consciousness sweeping over the whole continent, which were the radiating energy of the thoughts of those who existed on those planes.

He saw the highest of the planes bathed in a brilliance of light, which became progressively less as it passed down through the lower planes, where its positive life-sustaining energy was slowly being replaced by negative emotion. He saw that the Earth Plane was only one step away from the Underworld, and this closeness greatly troubled Thoth, because he could see that the two dark levels, on which the Underworld exists, were so full of destructive emotional thoughts such as anger, selfishness and even hate, that they were completely without light.

Knowing that no negative energy could harm him, Thoth began his journey by moving into the lower one of the two Dark Worlds. He wanted to know what life was like in these negative places. First, he needed time to adjust his energy to this cold, empty, dark and featureless world.

There was nothing there, everything had been destroyed by the negative and selfish thoughts of the people who existed in this place. The dark souls who exist here were hiding in caves, waiting to attack each other in fear and mistrust. Along the walls and floor slithered a dark glistening green slime, which Thoth knew to be the independent energy of evil.

Through the confusion of shouting, crying and profanities of every kind, Thoth saw five Spirits of Light moving silently and unseen through the darkness of the caves and hollow spaces. They were careful not to be caught in the webs of greed, vengeance and hate that had brought the inhabitants to this cold and lifeless place.

The Spirits of Light explained to Thoth that they were listening for small voices, crying out for help. Souls who had realised that there must be a better way to exist than in the dark depths of this unforgiving world of selfishness. When they heard such prayers for help, they would lift the suffering soul out of the depths of its misery and up into the next level of existence.

This level, though still dark and part of the Underworld, was like a bright light to those freshly out of the deep dark. From here the lost souls would, by their own thoughts, slowly work themselves out of the negative Dark and into brighter spheres. But it is a long and slow journey back to the Light for any soul that had allowed itself to fall that low.

Thoth noticed that both of these lower dimensions

were kept away from the main body of the Atlantean Continent by a powerful energy, which was easy enough to fall through, but exceedingly difficult to emerge from.

The Flood

Through the ages, Thoth watched as the radiating light separating the planes from one another became stronger. The highest of the planes continued to shine with a brightness beyond the comprehension of mankind, while the lowest, the Earth Plane, became darker and more resistant to the vibrations of the brilliant spheres above.

The light-sustaining energy of awareness, which invigorates every plane of Atlantis, became unable to penetrate the Darkness surrounding the Earth because of the negative attitudes people had developed towards each other in their emotionally filled lives. Due to the lack of the stimulating Light, on which all existence relies, the minds of the people on Earth were dulled and their souls fell into a semi-sleep state.

As a result, people started to rely more and more on emotional energy to sustain them through life. But negative emotional energy is not self-sustaining in the way that light-energy is, and so the years between birth and death became progressively shorter. Thoth saw that when the energy of a plane was not sufficient enough to sustain a long life, the sleeping soul would leave its body early, as in death, and move into the spheres between the planes. There they would remain suspended in a space between Earth and Atlantis, cared for by guiding souls who were from the higher realms of Atlantis.

These Spirit Guides, whom some of us often refer to as Guardian Angels, were responsible for making the souls aware of mistakes in the lives they had just completed and showing them a vision of the unnecessary hurt or difficulties they had caused for themselves and others. Based on the past and its mistakes, their next life was planned and organised, which would give them an opportunity to put right the hurt and wrongs they had committed, and to relive missed opportunities and grow away from self-interest and intolerance.

Based on the energy they had become, those who had caused deliberate acts of violence and destruction, would find themselves attracted to one of the two dark Underworlds, when life had finished. But the time between lives was not going to be easy or an enjoyable resting period for anyone who had deliberately hurt others. Instead, it would be a time of regret, living amongst others with a similar destructive and selfish energy as themselves, which allowed them to see who they had become.

Those who had become emotionally dependent on the energy of an addiction, would be unable to pull away from the negative influence in their lives and remain close to whatever it was they were addicted to. To be unseen by those still living, but moving amongst them as if they were ghosts, is perhaps the worst of all states. To be in the world, but not part of it, to be unable to have what you most crave and to be totally ignored by what or who you desire, is an indescribable agony.

Such as those who were unable to let go of their emotional desires, because of attachment, or with a need to control and impose their will on others, would remain close to the Earth until their emotional life-force would pull them back to begin a new life. These souls had lost the ability to choose for themselves, when to return to an earthly experience. They had forgotten their own laws of unselfish living, which would have taken them into a higher world when life had finished, and with that they had lost the balance that holds all life to the higher planes of ethereal Atlantis.

Those who had struggled to stay with the Light and lived an unselfish life, were lifted to the higher levels when life on Earth had finished. These higher levels are where fear is unknown, and where an exhausted soul could recover.

By this time, the Earth had lost its original beauty which Thoth had known in his youth: a time past and too distant to recall, while the Masters in the higher planes continued to expand the beauty and innocence of Atlantis, using the Flame of Life that was in their care.

Watching from his place above all planes the Great Lord, the highest Lord of All, became concerned that the negative emotions of the Earth were disturbing the balance of the whole continent, all ten Planes of Atlantis. He therefore directed the Masters of Life to separate the Earth from the other planes, so that the Earth's negative energies would no longer be able to interfere with the beauty and expansion of the higher planes.

In accordance with the laws that sustain all things, the Masters did as they were instructed and changed the direction of the Eternal Flame, so that the Earth would no longer be sustained by the full strength of the force that radiated from the heights of Atlantis. Without this supporting energy, the Earth and everything on the same level in the universe of which it was part became unbalanced, causing the seas to flood the land and all that was on it to disappear under water.

This is how the lowest of the planes, in which the planet Earth with its many spheres exists, became separated from the Paradise of Atlantis. And when the separation was complete, only a thin thread of awareness would remain to indicate a connection with Great Atlantis. Through this whole process the vibration of the lowest plane became slower and with that it became firm, more solid than it used to be. Matter became hard and unforgiving.

AFTER THE FLOOD

AFTER THE EARTH PLANE had separated from the main body of the Atlantean Continent the world became unstable. Oscillating and spiralling, the seas flooded the land and all life was lost. There was nothing left alive except for some form of smallest awareness. After eons of time and many more floods the Earth began to stabilise, allowing the rise and fall of many lifeforms to evolve – some so large that they were too big to last. But eventually, a balanced natural structure established itself and the planet Earth slowly evolved to a state where human life began to develop.

After the floods and while new levels of animal life were still finding their place, nature's vegetable world had taken over the planet. Vegetable awareness had endured through millions of years of heat, cold, wet and dry.

It was in the evolution of plants that the first of sustainable life evolved. First, from the tiny spores which floated on the winds grew the wonder-world of ferns, in all their varieties and shapes. Some of them were large enough to be above the reach of the animal world, and others so small as to be unseen by the insect world.

The soul of the vegetable world evolved to become the owner of this wet and then dry, unstable planet. Thoth had watched all the changes which had come to Planet Earth and knew that the memory of Earth's position on the Continent of Atlantis had not been forgotten and lay dormant in the developing awareness of nature's heart.

The time came when the Lord of All called Thoth back to the Temple of Light. He was told that the time had come to lead others down to Earth, to help open the hearts and minds of the new evolving human race in the ways of spiritual law. It was time to guide and instruct the emerging new races of people.

Thoth, and those he had chosen for this task, were to travel from Atlantis down to Earth by using the temple vortex, which had continued to exist, though unseen, beneath the sand and sea. Travelling in a vehicle of translucent energy through the unseen vortex, Thoth and his team arrived on Earth, where the lowest form of human life was slowly beginning to develop. They arrived in a place that was lush and green and had all that was necessary for the beginnings of a new human race.

These beginnings of human life more closely resembled animal awareness than anything resembling the humankind they were destined to become. Using the power of his energy, Thoth was able to unlock the potential of human awareness that was carried deep in the hearts of these new people. Because of what Thoth and the other Masters were able to do and teach, they quickly gained the confidence of the people, who believed that Thoth and the others were gods, descended from another place, another world.

Thoth sent the Masters who had journeyed with him to different parts of the Earth wherever life existed, to guide and teach the emerging human race in the ways that would lead them back to Atlantis. He quickly established a new kingdom at the place of their first arrival, which rose from its early beginnings of savagery to be an ordered civilized state.

Thoth realised from the beginning that if he were to instruct a race of people, so they were able to connect with the Planes of Atlantis, he would have to help them to evolve spiritually. They would need to develop a higher state of awareness and imagination than the one of fear and desire they were living in, if they were going to connect with the higher Realms of Light. Because the vibrations of energy on the Earth Plane were too slow to connect with any awareness of a higher plane, the new people on Earth would have to learn how to increase their own awareness and imagination to reconnect with the Soul of Atlantis.

Every plane, as well as every planet, has spaces within itself referred to as the *"Halls of Amenti"*. They are the soul of the plane or planet, and every Amenti is unique to the plane or planet it supports. The higher planes have much faster vibrations, and it was a connection to the supporting energy of the higher planes that Thoth needed for the emerging human race to develop. People's awareness needed to become more positive and creative and less negative and destructive, if they were going to be guided back onto the Continent of Atlantis, back into Paradise.

Thoth would have to teach these people how to work together and use their minds and their imagination to harness the power of nature through the sun, the water and the wind. But first, he needed them to know the importance of understanding the needs of nature, and how nature is as important to mankind as mankind is to nature. The two need each other and it would be foolish to ignore the unspoken intelligence and strength of the natural world.

As Thoth pointed out: the natural world has experienced survival through millions of years of adversity, and mankind was going to need and understand that experience if it was to advance to being more than a wild barbaric species.

Thoth started his new project by descending into the Halls of Amenti, or spaces within the Earth, which is where the energy of nature's awareness and vitality, in all its various forms and shapes, is held as a reservoir of memory. Nature's life has no separate or individual memory and relies on what has been before, as a collective memory, for its strength and continuous existence. This collective memory is shared by everything of the same species.

The planet develops and expands because of nature's memory, and it was here that Thoth needed to go if he were to understand all that exists and has ever existed on Earth. He needed to go into the heart of the planet, into its soul, and the spaces within it, the Halls of Amenti.

These halls are not areas that physical humans could enter into, or even find. They are a vibrating energy which is above human perception, and because mankind does not know of them he cannot interact with them. Neither can he destroy them with negative thinking.

It is into such spaces that insect and vegetable awareness go when their physical lives have finished. It was into the Earth's Halls of Amenti that Thoth needed to go to bring the memory of Atlantis' past to the surface, to accelerate the speed of human development. He knew the law.

Anything created, cannot be uncreated.
It continues to exist in the reservoirs of memory,
deep in the Soul of the Plane.

It is from these spaces, these Halls of Amenti, that the energy of life is drawn when needed. It is a reservoir of life-energy, drawn from all that has ever lived, but is now at rest. This life-force is held in readiness until it is needed by the seed of any new life, which is stimulated to grow.

All insect and vegetable awareness is drawn from the Soul of the Earth, and if the Halls of Amenti were to empty, nature would disappear. It is true to say that the Amenti are the heart of everything we call nature, and nature draws on the energy of life which is stored deep in these Earth spaces.

The Halls of Amenti are the library of the planet's soul, where all known and gathered information of life on Earth is stored for eternity. When the physical existence of a plant, animal, insect, or any other form of the millions of different varieties on Earth can no longer be sustained, its life-force is drawn back into the reservoir from which it came. The entire life-experience of the individual becomes one with all the other memories which are already stored, so that what has been experienced during a life-time as a member of nature's community on the surface of the planet will not be lost, but become shared information for future lives and experiences.

No experience is ever wasted and Thoth had many times gone into the souls of the different planes and planets, to learn about the life-energy that is stored there. It was here that he learned how to raise his vibrations to see the collective energy of the past in action. He watched the plants and saw that within and around the individual plant were many other plants of the same species. They were all existing in the same energy of the one living the experience, but adding to it, not drawing from it.

This energy, drawn from the reservoir of memory in the Halls of Amenti, is a supporting energy without which no plant would survive for very long. It acts as the essence of life, and it is exactly the same for all life. The purer the atmosphere through which the plant is living, the more of this supporting energy the plant is able to access to enhance the living experience, which is why in a pure environment the plants and other life forms look healthy and vibrant. In a polluted or disturbed environment on the other hand, nature lacks the strength and vibrant colours of its true potential.

It is because mankind has lost its trust in what it cannot see or experience that it has become such a lonely individual on this plane, unable to communicate with other life-forces who share the same space, and to live up to its full potential. Life is so much shorter and far more difficult than it needs to be. If humanity could understand the important role of nature in its experience on Earth, life would be longer, healthier and happier.

If people would only use the same natural resources that are stored in the soul of the planet instead of destroying and polluting what they do not understand, the planet and all life on it would benefit, including mankind. This is why Thoth found the need for people to know the significance of understanding the needs of nature as well as their own so important.

Nature gets its strength from a shared identity with all other life that is living on the planet, and also from that which has ceased to live, but continues to exist as memory. Nothing is ever lost, even though mankind has lost the ability to share nature's strength as well as the experiences of all different members of its own race.

How much healthier and happier they were in the days of Atlantis, when people knew the importance of bonding with all life that shared the same space. They were stronger in those times because of their shared differences and knew that they would become weaker if they ceased to share, in a need to feel superior.

For his mission, Thoth was binding the people together as one, knowing from what he had seen in nature that shared knowledge is strength. It was from the shared experience of multiple past lives, including his own, that mankind would grow. It was not only a shared experience with its own species, but also an awareness of the importance of understanding what other species had learned that needed to be acknowledged.

Many species of animal and plant life have knowledge and experiences from beyond this plane, which they would share if mankind were to raise its awareness and reach out for help from the kingdom of nature, instead of treating all other life on Earth as some sort of sub-species lacking awareness, which they need to dominate.

Thoth recalled the times when Earth was still part of Atlantis, a paradise, where all life existed as one. A time when awareness was a shared experience and the plants, the animals, the seas, the weather and people were all one, and no one thought of ownership or supremacy. A time when every species knew the value of a shared existence and avoided the fear that is born from superiority and desire, causing separateness.

Emotion in Place

Thoth saw that it was the Earth's slow vibration, caused by negative emotion, which was blocking a closer connection between human life and similar life on the higher planes. He realised that if he was going to succeed in raising this new human race to its heights, it needed to ascend, and he would have to teach people how to avoid or overcome the negativity which now dominated their thinking.

The low vibration caused by expressions of negative emotion, was holding the Earth and its people to the darker spheres. It cannot be otherwise. It is spiritual law that awareness and acceptance of all life, equally and without fear, desire, or superiority, raises humanity above the negative emotions of destructive thinking. The fear referred to is that of an avoidable negative emotion such as doubt, worry or uncertainty, and not anticipated violence, or trauma, from situations that are beyond personal control.

Thoth knew that he had to introduce a form of spirituality into the awareness of mankind if he was to succeed in giving humanity an opportunity to ascend to higher Levels of Light. But first, he must bond the human race as a living unit of one mind.

At the time of Thoth's arrival on the material plane of the Earth, the driving force of survival had been the negative energies of fear for life, desire for whatever passed as security, and superiority as a natural need for leaders. This resulted in competition, with the strongest taking the most and the best of whatever was available.

At this early stage in the development of the human race, the higher vibrations of shared values and trust was an unknown force outside nature. It was the power of sharing and selflessness that Thoth was going to introduce. His task was to raise humanity above the negativity that covered the Earth Plane and back to the Levels of Light, which are above the negative emotions of self-centred survival. Only when humans had overcome their basic negative emotions, could Thoth begin to think of moving them through the protective and powerful light-barrier that separates the higher planes of Atlantis from the Earth.

In his observations on the development of humanity,

Thoth explains in his records the necessity of overcoming the barriers of negative emotion, of becoming one with the soul of the planet, to reach the levels of contentment and beauty that exist in the World of Nature. It was this that he was bringing to the surface of human awareness.

Once the individual had conquered his or her emotional blocks, they would begin to experience a greater force than their own. When people became equal to the natural forces, the power of their shared awareness would begin to release them from their prison of negativity.

This was the secret of Atlantis' success, peace, and contentment: in tune with the power of the natural forces. Rather than destroying nature's balance and harmony or trying to control it, the Atlanteans nurtured it and with that they released and increased their own power.

This is what frees the soul to move on to higher planes of the Light. Until humans can become masters of their emotions, they live in a sleep-state, almost zombie-like and less than fully aware, under the controlling influence of negative emotion. In death, awareness returns to what it should have been.

This waking-up of consciousness after life can be quite a shock to some, who come to realise what they have done, or not done, while they were *sleep-living*. The level of awareness one reaches in the Afterlife depends on how well the emotions have been managed, or eliminated, during the time on Earth. And, unless the emotions are thoroughly in check, people will be born to die again and again, until they begin to overcome their negative and selfish attitudes.

Those who live by the energy of destructive emotions, such as jealousy and corruption, move themselves by their own thoughts down towards one of the two darker Underworlds.

Thoth had begun his work to bring the savage race of people, lacking any form of trust, out of Darkness and into the Light and described his purpose for descending to Earth in his records. The Spirits of Light knew that the expanding human race, locked in negative thoughts, could not evolve into an autonomous creative force until the negative force was neutralised. Therefore, one of the first things they did was to increase the force of vision and imagination amongst people. This had the effect of protecting the evolving human race from the overpowering forces of destructive thinking.

Inspired imagination is a driving force in the development of humanity, which neutralises the negativity in the emotions that would otherwise act as a brake on the work that Thoth had set himself to do. It is through imagination that the Masters can, and do, control the speed at which humanity evolves. If for example one section of society is evolving faster than another, they will simply withhold the inspiration of imagination from this one section and increase it in the other. When the Masters withhold inspiration from either an individual or a whole section of society, negativity starts to creep back in.

At any rate, it was only after the introduction of inspired imagination that humanity began to evolve more quickly than the World of Nature. By using the force of imagination and inspiring it in the direction the Masters wanted to guide humanity, Thoth and his companions were able to develop in a few hundred years, what would have taken thousands and thousands of years, if ever, had mankind been left to evolve at the pace of nature.

The Masters of Light guided the evolving thoughts of this new human race to create great civilisations, of which traces can still be found in many parts of the world today. With a growing awareness of self-worth, beauty, feelings of sensitivity and other positive thoughts, men's creative imagination began to flourish.

Humanity quickly rose from its early unimaginative and barbaric way of living, to become the great civilisations of antiquity. Working through Thoth, the Masters had used the forces of positive emotional energy, which is active only for as long as it is driven by inspired imagination. Negative emotion on the other hand has always been the brake on human development.

Thus, the Masters also increased the density of the veil between the living and those who had died, but who continued to exist as a negative force, influencing the thoughts of the living. While people dying with positive energy had freed themselves from many of the negative forces and were attracted directly into a higher level of the Astral World, those dying with addictions, desires or fears, were held close to the Earth's low vibrational field and the lower levels of the Astral World.

The thoughts of these negative people were a disturbance on the positive influence that Thoth and the Spirits of Light were developing for a speedy construction of a new civilisation. This was the reason to increase the density of the veil between the Earth and the After Life.

In conclusion, the Masters were able to inspire mankind to ensure a continuous evolution through their growing awareness of spirituality, with ideas of beauty and art in their many forms. The power of positive imagination, which flows through all the planes of Atlantis, was now connected with the planet Earth.

The aim was that people would be able to lift themselves to the highest status of awareness and creativity possible, and become responsible for their own search for the perfection of the soul, to finally regain their rightful place on Atlantis.

PYRAMIDS OF ATLANTIS

THOTH EXPLAINS THAT the highest of the ten planes of Atlantis is surrounded by the energy of the lesser bright planes, or realms, that make up the continent. The whole arrangement is in the shape of a pyramid, with the darkest and least evolved plane being on the outer and lower ring of the design. Between each plane there is an energy field[3], which prevents anything not equal to the density and vibration of the higher plane from passing through. This is to protect the lesser evolved souls from the intensity of the energy at the higher levels.

The higher planes appear to be smaller than those below, but this is only because of the intensity of the energy in the mass. All energy moves in spirals and as the energy intensifies and quickens the spiral becomes narrower, creating the shape of a pyramid. Everything within a plane is vibrating at a higher level of creative imagination than the one below it.

---

[3] Thoth used the pictogram of *'waves'* to explain this energy field, as a symbol. The symbol generally indicates *'energy'* and depends on the context.

The higher the plane, the more intense the creative abilities of awareness and imagination. Living through an intense energy is not much different to living in a less intense energy because your thoughts will have come into harmony with the energy surrounding you. However, space and time are quite different, which is why it is so difficult to communicate between the different planes.

Every plane has its own time and space awareness, depending on the intensity of the plane's energy. Yet it is only when you move from one plane to another that you notice the difference. This is because the souls living through the faster energy have increased the intensity of their own energy to be in harmony with the plane they have moved into, which happens when they become more positive in every area of their awareness.

Souls are only able to enter into a higher plane when they have completed the lessons that were set for them by the Masters of Light. Lessons meant to teach the laws of spirituality, which you would need to understand if you were to rise above earthly awareness.

Once you have moved out of the Earth Plane, you are taught how to work and create with thought-energy, how to construct images using imagination and how to move with your mind so that travel becomes a thought-motivated movement. Constructing things with energy is quite different to using solid materials as we do on Earth. It is less cumbersome and there are no tools because you are constructing, shaping, or building with your mind.

The list of lessons is endless and beyond the imagination of human awareness. It is important to understand that the more positive you are, and the more knowledge you acquire, the more intense your energy becomes. Three factors: knowledge, a positive attitude and unselfish consciousness intensify the energy, allowing you to come into harmony with the higher vibrations of the next plane.

Any soul wanting to move away from the Wheel of Rebirth needs to increase the intensity of their energy with positive, constructive thinking. Any negativity such as doubts, fixed ideas or any form of emotionally based attitudes, will hold you to the lower Worlds of Creation.

This is why mankind has so much difficulty getting out of the rebirth cycle. They seem unable to understand that it is negative emotion that holds them to the slower vibrations of the Earth. To ascend, they need to become positive and emotionally free of all attachments, which will otherwise magnetically attract them back into the type of life they have just left.

To move into higher levels of awareness does not mean that your personality is lost, but it needs to change and grow in integrity if you are going to get off the Wheel of Rebirth and move up into the higher Planes of Light. It is the same within all levels of awareness.

Every plane is like a different country, each one more

beautiful and inspiring than the previous one, but also requiring higher levels of integrity. The difference between one dimension and the next is the intensity of the energy and it is easier to move down the scale than it is to move up, as it is easier to be emotionally negative than positive.

Thoth tells us that there are nine Masters responsible for keeping the balance between the different planes. Two of whom are responsible for keeping the two Underworlds, which are dark with negativity, from encroaching into the higher planes. The seven remaining Masters are responsible for guiding the souls from the lowest plane to the highest level of awareness. There is a controlling Master for every level of the Atlantean Continent, or Pyramid, except for the highest plane where the Lord of All dwells.

There are further Masters at every level who watch over and guide the countless souls, as they work to ascend from one level to the next. No one is left to struggle on their own and communication between Master and pupil is from mind to mind. This is the voice you sometimes hear in your head, warning you when you are about to do something which you know is wrong or, when an inspirational idea just suddenly pops into your thoughts. It is the same energy that guides you to find the perfect job, or house, or friend.

The same energy is responsible for all those little

coincidences in your life. Those who are free of doubt and believe that their life is directed from a higher level and are prepared to follow what they feel, will be directed from the beginning of their lives through to the end. It is when logic, doubt or emotions get in the way of common sense that spiritual communication breaks down.

It is further impossible to have any thought that would not be heard by someone, at some level. Of course, this means that there are no secrets between this and the higher worlds, and once you leave this world whatever you are thinking is immediately understood by whoever or whatever the thought refers to.

In the higher worlds you also see with your mind. So, whatever you are thinking will be seen and heard by everyone in the radius of your thoughts. This is how nature and the animal world communicate, they create a picture in their mind of the thought they want to communicate. This way is much more efficient than using our limited vocabulary. As someone once said, 'A picture is worth a thousand words.'

It is not possible to move off the Wheel of Rebirth before you have your thoughts and emotions under control. You would not be allowed into a situation where you would embarrass yourself, which is yet another reason for learning to control your thoughts and emotions.

What Thoth means to explain is that energy moves in vibrating spirals and the spirals appear to move either up or down, depending on your thoughts. If you are positive the spirals will be turning around to the right and up, if you are having negative thoughts the spirals will turn to the left and down. In a pyramid formation, the energy of a spiral becomes more intense towards the apex, which is where the energy is concentrated.

To move up through the planes, the individual's control over emotional and negative thinking needs to improve, so that one comes into harmony with the increasing intensity of the positive energy of the higher plane. This is why it is so difficult for anyone with negative thoughts to evolve from one level to the next and move off the Wheel of Rebirth. Because unless all emotional thoughts are at least under control and the individual is in harmony with the unselfish positive energy of inspirational creativity, free of all destructive thoughts, they will continue to reincarnate into the lower and heavier human form.

In the higher planes of Atlantis there is no specific time or space as we understand it. It is the positive power of imagination, through awareness, that holds the individual soul to any specific space. Each Master on every plane is responsible for allowing an individual soul to move on. Once the soul has harmonised with the new world, he or she will be guided to further improve on what they have already become.

In short, nothing happens on its own and the arrangement of the spiritual world is no different. Every plane is managed and controlled to ensure it remains in balance with those above or below. It was because the Earth became overweighed with negative energy that it separated from the worlds above. It is this balance that Thoth had set himself to correct, after he had met with the highest Lord, the Great Lord.

It was because of Thoth's persistent search for knowledge, in awareness and imagination, that he was released from the bonds of any particular plane and allowed to travel anywhere within the pyramid formation of Atlantis. It was explained to him that he was free to search for wisdom wherever he wanted to go, in any of the spheres. He was given the choice of remaining in the highest of the planes or moving to any other plane that he chose to explore.

In any case, at the end of his search for wisdom he would have to choose some form of work, because all souls must forever continue to learn, teach or work, which usually means helping the souls on a lower plane. It was explained to Thoth, that even though he had reached the Heights of Atlantis, by doing so he had only pushed the peak of the mountain of knowledge and wisdom, for which he was searching, higher. There will always be higher levels and greater knowledge to aim for, even higher than the tenth plane of Atlantis.

In reality, Thoth had gained just one step on the long path to infinite wisdom. Now that he was free to choose for himself what to do, he decided to work with the Masters, bringing Light to the evolving human race on Earth. He was shown how to search for the mysteries of life in the Halls of Amenti.

He was told that he would need to understand awareness and creative imagination in all its forms, if he was going to bring a sense of spirituality and integrity to the rising race of humanity.

Structure of Atlantis

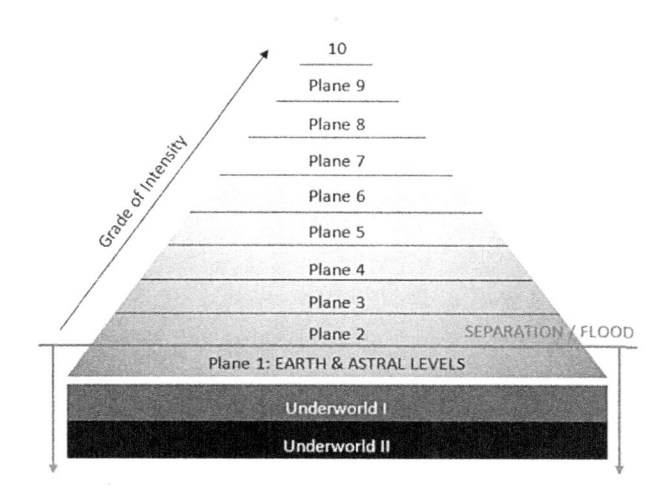

```
                              10
                           Plane 9
                           Plane 8
                           Plane 7
   Grade of Intensity      Plane 6
                           Plane 5
                           Plane 4
                           Plane 3
                           Plane 2       SEPARATION / FLOOD
                    Plane 1: EARTH & ASTRAL LEVELS
                         Underworld I
                         Underworld II
```

LORD LIFE AND DEATH

BEFORE BEGINNING HIS TASK, Thoth was led into a great space which, although filled with Light, was shrouded in Darkness. The space in which he found himself was ruled by the Lord responsible for Life and Death. Nothing happens on Earth that is not seen and monitored at a higher level.

Thoth had been taken into this space by a Master, and in the centre of the hall he tells us, '…was a great figure of night, darker than darkness.'

After a while the Master spoke to the Lord of Darkness, explaining that Thoth had been granted freedom from death. The Master explained that Thoth had been granted Eternal Life and was to be freed from the Cycle of Rebirth. The Lord of Life and Death then shone a great energy of light from his hand which filled the hall, and the Veil of Darkness lifted away.

It was then that Thoth was able to see millions of lights. The souls, he was told, of every life. Some larger, some smaller, some bright, others only radiating a dim glow. Some were close, while others were far in the distance.

Around every light he saw a Veil of Darkness, preventing the light from escaping, so that the millions of lights hung like illumined little orbs in the sky. And although in some the spark was small and distant, it was explained to him that every soul is a light that could never be extinguished, since:

What has been created, cannot be uncreated.

The Lord of Life and Death explained that the lights were the souls of men, showing how some grow and others fade, and although they might become just a speck of light surrounded by deep darkness, no light is ever extinguished. The soul is eternal, and even when they are covered in the dark of selfishness and destruction, fear or sadness, they will exist forever. Constantly changing, but continuously living through the dark, in both Life and Death, until they realise that there is a better way, and force themselves through positive awareness and determination, to become a brighter light.

He went on to explain how, when a soul had reached the fullness of its light, it would change to reappear in another form, so that through eons all life, from the lowest to the highest level of awareness, will evolve to become a greater form. Each time growing until the soul is ready to move on. Death comes, but like sleep never remains. Life always returns to conquer the Darkness until the soul is ready to move into greater levels of awareness.

Then Thoth saw how one of the lights separated from the others, shining and expanding with brightness until the whole hall was filled with its unique glow. In the quiet the Lord of Darkness spoke, *'See your own soul, Thoth, as it grows in light. You are now free, forever, from the Lord of the Night.'*

The Master then took Thoth through many great spaces which were filled with mysteries, known only to the Masters. Mysteries and wisdom, he was told, that mankind can never know until they have also conquered all negative thought, and become an awareness of creative imagination, free from their heavy bodies.

They space-travelled until Thoth was brought before the Lords, and he knelt before them. He was asked what work he intended to do, now that he had become a Spirit of Light.

Thoth asked to be allowed to be a teacher to the new human race that was evolving on the lost plane of Atlantis, on the planet Earth. He said that he wanted to instruct and guide the developing human race until they too were lights among life.

After some consideration the Lord of All proclaimed that it was decreed that Thoth was to be a Master of Men, that he had made this his destiny. He was to take his power and wisdom, and shine a spark of light into the new human race, to guide and help them to grow and evolve, to become free of the negative and destructive thoughts that hold all life to Darkness.

Light and Dark

Throughout his writings Thoth refers to the "*Light*" and its opposite, the "*Dark*", and so we need to understand exactly what he means by these two terms. He says we *are* the soul, which is another word for spirit or awareness, and that without awareness we wouldn't even know that we exist.

It's natural to want to be more than we already are. This means that we also need an imagination, without which nothing happens. We don't grow spiritually if we don't do something to make it happen. From helping the neighbours to deciding what to do for ourselves, nothing can happen without the ability to visualise a creative action, or a situation in the future.

From this you will realise that the soul is a combination of two forces: awareness and creative imagination. Both of them rely on the force of a balanced energy, positive and negative, while they are living through a physical experience. The soul begins its journey as a creative thought in the highest of all minds, and has since the beginning travelled for eons through many species and different forms of life, to become spiritually evolved into human form. Inherent in the depths of every soul are thoughts of creativity, beauty, peace, innocence and faith.

The soul knows that all creations of life are equally valued, from plants through animals to people, though in different ways. The soul is an awareness of creative energy, and is mainly concerned with a life of learning and experiencing, to grow in awareness and wisdom. It has no need to be seen, to have, to dominate or to control. This radiating creative energy of the soul is what Thoth refers to as the *"Light"*.

Now enters an alien force: emotion. Emotion is inherently destructive as it depends on the energy of others for its survival. Its need for energy is excessive and greedy. It depletes energy reserves wherever it finds it, and then, out of fear, it destroys whatever it thinks might harm or oppose it.

Emotion is a totally separate force and therefore not part of the soul. However, it negatively overwhelms the individual soul to block any form of positive or creative thinking to stay in control. This greedy, demanding and sometimes passive energy is what prevents the soul from coming into its full potential, as a creative and imaginative power.

Similar to parasites living in the body, emotions feed on the positive energy of their host. They spread quickly from one person to the next, and once you have them they are very difficult to dislodge. Unless prevented from doing so, emotions will grow to influence your every thought and action, and because of their excessive need for energy they disturb the body's negative-positive balance, disproportionally increasing the negative polarity by consuming the available positive energy.

As a result, the body is often out of balance, lacking the positive energy that was taken by emotion. This causes all sorts of health and attitude problems such as stress-related illnesses, a weak immune system, depression, etc.

Emotion weakens the life-force of its potential for happiness and contentment, which in turn leads to selfish attitudes and a need to surround itself with more of everything, to increase security and superiority to control its situation. As we age, emotional needs become a drain on the fitter and younger people around us, as the body tries to maintain its electromagnetic balance. This of course, robs other people of their positive energy.

Emotion always puts itself first if it can, to ensure its own survival, no matter what it claims its intention to be. Which is why even when people are seemingly doing something for others, there will be an underlying selfish need to satisfy a certain emotion.

Everything about emotion is competitive. It is selective in its attitude towards others and prefers situations it thinks to be beneficial to its own interests, and rejects anything or anyone who it believes might oppose it, or take from it desperately needed energy.

Any situation in your mind which is selective i.e., 'I

like this person, but not that one,' is a thought from your emotional mind, and not from your soul. Emotion always puts its own needs first, and the more you are in the grip of emotion, the more obvious this becomes. Emotion is a destructive and abusive force, dominating the soul and feeding on the positive energy of its host as well as others.

This is what Thoth refers to as the "*Dark*".

It is dark because emotion absorbs positive energy in its selfish attempt for survival. It sucks all power out of the life-force, which relies on light-energy. In spiritual terms the body is unimportant, except as a temporary shell which moves the soul from place to place. We truly are body, mind and spirit (Body, Emotion and Soul). [4]

Thoth begins his seventh tablet by emphasising the importance of living life through the positive energy of the Light because this is the only way to wisdom, and of course, positive thoughts stimulate us with restorative energy.

He is also very aware that life's journey is full of problems, which are sure to be full of temptations towards the selfish side of life. He insists that we must look for the Way to the Light, which is our Soul Path. We should always seek to do what we know in our

---

[4] The role of emotion and how it affects the health of mind and body is thoroughly discussed in my earlier book 'You and Your Mobile Home'.

hearts to be right because the Way of the Light is eternal, whereas the Life in Darkness is limited.

Anyone, he tells us, who favours negative emotion gives the dark forces power, which will return them time and again back to rebirth, to begin life over again. Once we give the Dark an expression or personality, it will not let go of us easily.

It is only when we overcome the temptations and illusions of the Dark Path that we gain the strength to live in the Light and become free of the problems of life on Earth. We are only separated from peace, contentment and spiritual awareness by our own negative emotions. Once we have the negative energies under control, we can begin to enjoy the more positive and light-filled spaces of our existence.

Light fills all the planes above the Astral World, and no dark energy is allowed through from the Astral into the World of Atlantis. So, if you are carrying any selfish or negative thoughts, you will not be able to enter the higher planes of light.

To escape from the earth-bound struggles of life and end the Cycle of Rebirth, you need to be free of the attractions that hold you to this Earth. Attractions to anything such as money, home, family, pleasure, revenge, anger, fear, security… Whatever you think it is that you cannot live without, will hold you to the Wheel of Rebirth.

Around and around you go, life after life, death after

death, getting nowhere because you refuse to let go the illusion of emotional need. Emotions which you think are essential for happiness will ensure that you will be back when life has finished, to begin all over again, not realising that you are being withheld from the beauty and freedom of spiritual life by your own doing.

It's an emotional illusion to think you cannot manage without this or that, which keeps you tied as a slave to the hard and unforgiving world of substance, a life you so desperately refuse to leave behind.

You cannot enter into the higher worlds of the Light, carrying any baggage of negative emotion. There is nothing of this world that has any value in the higher realms. So, we are told to ignore that which our hearts know to be wrong. We are told not to be concerned with what others have, do, or say because this is only a trap to keep us in the negative thoughts of the Dark.

Even when life seems to have closed out any chance of light, know that if you search for it, you will find it. Love is all around, and by keeping the mantra *I Love You* constantly in your thoughts, you will make sure to keep that connection.

'Sing it for the ones you love.

'Sing it for the ones in need of help.

'Sing it for the ones who oppose you.'

But most of all, 'Sing it for the light in your soul, the child you are.'

Everything created is based on order, on cosmic laws,

and Thoth tells us that all order is held in the Eternal Flame. An energy that is the power, which holds all the worlds together. Without this Flame of Light, the power of creativity that flows through everything, there would be nothing but chaos. Darkness being the master of chaos.

Balance on the other hand keeps chaos away, and relies on the cosmic laws that flow from the topmost plane of Atlantis down through to the Earth Plane. The planes rely on the laws and their acceptance, to preserve all that is. It has been this way since the beginning and will continue without end.

The search to know more about life and its purpose should be constantly in our thoughts. The more we learn, the more we will come to the realisation that there is always more to learn. And Thoth tells us that the Lord said to him:

'If you want wisdom – seek it in the Flame of Light.
'If you want knowledge – seek it in the Flame of Light.
'If you want to be one with the Flame of Light – seek it within your own hidden flame.'

Thoth's Pathway to Light

For thousands upon thousands of years Thoth lived amongst people, both seen and unseen. Teaching and guiding them with his wisdom. He is a light that shines through all life, as it struggles to climb out of negative Darkness.

Then came the time when Thoth needed to return to the highest plane of Atlantis to restore his energy. He tells us that he has left a record of his teachings in the minds of mankind, and that they must guard his teachings well because they are the Keys to Eternal Life, the keys to overcoming the Cycle of Rebirth with its energy of negative emotion.

Thoth, now a Master from Atlantis, freely chose to share his wisdom and awareness with humanity that was slowly evolving on the Earth Plane. He knew it was his responsibility to ensure that this new race would grow, and to shine a light of creative awareness through the world to lift the darkness of negativity which had flooded the planet.

Thoth left a record explaining that wisdom is power, and power is wisdom, and together they overcome the negativity in awareness. Negativity, he explains, is the Darkness that bonds humanity to the Wheel of Rebirth, preventing it from lifting into the paradise of Atlantis.

He explains that any act of destruction or hurt creates a further Darkness around the soul, which is in direct conflict to its contentment and happiness. The Darkness quickly becomes stronger than the Light and it can take many lifetimes and hundreds of years, before the soul regains its original strength.

He knew that unless he left some rules his followers could refer to, they would soon forget what they had been taught and lose themselves in the midst of Darkness. He has therefore left a list of the following basic rules to help anyone who wants to end the Cycle of Rebirth, and lift away from the negative influences that prevent a return to the Worlds of Light. Rules that need to be read and reread, and thought about in the longer term, so that they become part of our awareness, part of our soul, to guide us onto the right path of enlightenment.

Here are his guidelines, but please note that for practical reasons the masculine pronoun has been used throughout.

'Don't be proud of what you know. The Wisdom of Atlantis would fill libraries, and although you have learned the first line of the first law, do not give yourself reason to believe you know them all. Listen to anyone who is brought to you as a teacher, they may not know what you know, but they will carry wisdom that is not yet in your heart.'

'Stay distant when you hear negativity, gossip and that which you know to be untrue. The Truth will shine through for those with wisdom, while those clothed in false words and thoughts will remain in the Dark.'

'If you should wander into thoughts of negativity, the laws of wisdom and truth will avoid you. Only through the law of positive thought will you find freedom from Darkness.'

'Be not the cause of fear, for fear binds men to the Darkness of Rebirth and you will be bound in the depth of darkness by the fear you have caused.'

'If frustration clouds your thoughts, remember that others might not be on your path and therefore, not see or feel what you see or feel.'

'Follow your heart through every lifetime. To go against what you know to be right or true, is to injure your soul. Never sin against your own integrity.'

'If you become rich, do what you know to be right. Riches will not heal a soul which lies dying in the Darkness of Regret.'

'Only your thoughts follow you into eternity. With your thoughts you will create a radiant bright body or a dark malevolent image, which will follow you as a light or a shadow into eternity.'

'If you follow the laws and do what your heart tells you is right, you will be guided along a straight path. But if you join with the emotional talk of others, the straight path will avoid you and become long and twisted.'

'The only truth worth knowing is about yourself. The only truth you can change is your own.'

'If you live and work amongst others, find someone whose heart follows the law. Love is the bond that strengthens the soul.'

'When someone comes for advice listen without judgement, so that they remain free of any guilt which would prevent them from learning and overcoming Darkness. If someone hesitates to confide in you, it is because you are at fault in your judgement of men.'

'Don't join in with negative attitudes, nor listen to them. Negative attitudes come from people or situations that are out of balance. If you stay quiet, they will know you have the Wisdom of Truth.'

'Silence is power. It causes the idle talker to listen to their own exaggeration, and they learn from themselves in your silence.'

'Refrain from boasting about what you have done, there will always be others who will claim to have done more, causing you to fall into the Negativity of Darkness.'

'Be known for your gentleness and tolerance, which comes from a heart that is full of light.'

'To know someone, spend time with them. Never take your opinion of someone or a situation from the thoughts of another.'

'Wisdom must always be shared. It is given to you in trust to help others.'

'Wisdom must not be shared with the doubters: it will emotionally hurt them. Those who doubt the Truth live in the Darkness of Sleep. They will neither hear nor see the Truth.'

'A wise man lets his heart overflow with the beauty of life, but stays silent to prevent disturbing its contentment.'

'Remember that awareness and imagination walk together, but imagination can be positive or negative.'

'Negative imagination binds man to the Darkness of Rebirth. Wisdom can only grow in awareness when imagination is positive.'

'Positive imagination is the most potent force of awareness because it overcomes all other forces, and penetrates all that is possible on Earth.'

'Always listen to the calm voice of reason and wisdom, it is inspiration from the Light. There are mysteries in Atlantis that when unveiled, will fill the world with light.'

'Let anyone who wants to be free from the Bondage of Darkness first separate the material from the immaterial, the earthly from the spiritual, knowing that earth returns to earth, and the spirit returns to spirit.'

'Those who aspire to be a Spirit of Light will ascend, and forever dwell in the Paradise of Atlantis. Those who believe in nothing will have nowhere to go.'

'Man grows from that which resists him. Therefore life must resist man, or he could not grow.'

'Do not question when someone sees a colour differently to yourself. Not everyone sees with the same eyes. That which they see will be attracting what they need to see.'

'Man is a Child of Light, burning bright through the night. A light that can never be quenched, even in a world of negativity, or under the Veil of Death.'

'In man's heart there is much stress because of negative thinking. Don't waste your power in maintaining

an energy that has no purpose.'

'Ask yourself: how long will you have your name and body? Only what you think, lives through all time and space.'

'Man is as a star bound to a body until by his own effort, he is freed to shine out in new life. He who searches for Truth in all things becomes free to shine through the Night that would hold him to Darkness.'

'All that exists is only another form of that which does not exist. Life is constantly changing. Try not to hold 'what is' for it will soon change to become 'what was', and nothing you can do will prevent it. Grasp what is to be, and release what is struggling to escape into past-time.'

'Wisdom comes from following the law of change, not fighting it. In the fullness of time you also will become a brighter star, grown out of Darkness to be a Star of the Light.'

'All through the ages the Light has been hidden behind the Darkness. Be free of illusion and walk in the Light to learn the mysteries of life that are hidden from men.'

WINDOWS OF THE MIND

IN HIS CHILDHOOD, LONG BEFORE the Earth became separated from the continent of Atlantis, Thoth used to sit beneath the stars, dreaming of the mysteries that lay in dimensions beyond his reach. He had a great longing to find the secret that was blocking his way to the higher worlds of greater knowledge.

Throughout his early years he sought the pathways that would lead to wisdom and the greater worlds of Atlantis. Eventually, he found a way to leave his physical body. In meditation he flew through the window of his mind, and into the night. That way he was free to find the wisdom that would unlock the secrets, which are withheld from mankind.

His soul travelled far into space, searching for knowledge that held the Mysteries of Life, while his body lay peacefully awaiting his return. He visited the planets, some of which were greater than it was possible to imagine. Only now, free of his body, could he see and know of the existing life on those planets, each of which consisted of many planes of their own.

There, in all his wanderings through space, he found the law that was working its beauty through the human race. Thoth had found the Plane of Harmony and Rhythm, which is the beating heart of everything. He experienced the pulse, the push and pull of the seasons as they came and went, in birth and death to be reborn again. He felt the rise and fall of the sun as day gave way to night, to begin again when night gave up its sleep to day. He saw, he felt, he heard, the rhythm of gain and loss, of coming and going to come again. He rose and fell through spirals of time, to rise again and know no end.

Thoth learned that nothing was lost, and nothing was gained. He marvelled at the beauty and contentment in all that existed and became one with the harmony of music, which is the Song of Great Atlantis. He sensed the fullness and balance of the harmony in the spiralling flow of the pulsing push and pull. There were neither thoughts nor words that could express what he was feeling. Awareness was in the harmonious beauty of the music of the spheres.

Thoth knew he had found one of the Three Keys of Wisdom.

♀ Total freedom from fear, a peace that transcends all peace.

A place, open only to those seeking contentment, but closed to those seeking pleasure. A place where fear is banned and only trust and love that is born from a heart that gives of itself to all that exists, can enter the secret door of this paradise.

Thoth continued his journey through the stars, where neither time nor space have meaning, and where awareness with imagination is everything. He visited planets and saw many types and forms of life. Some races of men so advanced, they had become a living brightness in their light. Others fallen so low in negativity that they lived in a world as dark as the night.

Wherever he went, all the life he encountered was either struggling to reach higher into the Light, or allowing itself to fall further into Darkness, but nowhere was life standing still. Even those who were living in the realms of illumination were looking for greater brightness.

Thoth saw that for awareness to live it had to keep moving. Motivated either by positive energy and lifting itself up into the Light, or by negative energy and forcing itself down into Darkness. He learned that there is only movement, back or forth, like the pendulum clock, for awareness will cease to be when the pendulum falls silent and still.

Thoth wanted humanity to know that the Light is its destiny, and that Darkness is no more than a negative veil across the mind, imprisoning the light of the soul and preventing its creative energy of imagination and happiness from being free to express itself.

During his search for the Keys of Wisdom, Thoth travelled through the different planes of Atlantis and found some people from far in the past, who had conquered space with flight while still living in a fixed form. They had found the secret of spiralling energy, and learned how to contain it as a positive force, a force that moves all things through all things. They had learned how to use the positive spiralling energy of life and light as a constructive force, to build and shape energy into structures that pleased the eyes, or in which to rest and contemplate the wonders of life.

Even in that time, when Earth was still part of Atlantis, this race of people had outstripped the science of all other races. These people were mighty in wisdom, they were truly Beings of Light. Thoth stayed a long time with this race of men to learn of their wisdom. He saw how they built great cities using minerals made from the base energy of all matter: imagination.

They created what they needed out of the positive free-flowing energy of the mind, through which they lived. They had learned how to conquer the elements by using the positive forces of awareness and imagination, and to bend the energies of space to their own will.

Thoth continued his journey through the different planes, seeing new things and old things, learning the different ways of many races of men on Atlantis. He learned that whichever plane or world you inhabit, you are like a star.

'Your body is a planet revolving around a central sun, your soul. And when you search for wisdom you become free to shine like a sun that others will follow. Your soul must ever move on, away from the Darkness and into the Light.'

He implores anyone reading the records of his search for wisdom to recognise that they are no more than an energy with awareness and imagination, they can grow out of darkness and struggle to become a light as bright as the sun. The sun was not something to pray to, but something to become.

Thoth, having seen the Wonders of Atlantis and knowing that his soul was free, even when his body was bound, wanted to know of the source of wisdom. This thought brought him to a plane that was new to him. It was the heart of the wisdom he had been searching for. He saw that life is not physical, but that life is truly the Light, which is in everything.

This is what every soul is constantly searching for, the source of wisdom that makes it one with all that is.

He learned that negativity is disorder and chaos, and that only through the order of spiritual law can one come into harmony and balance with all that exists. Anyone who wants to be one with all wisdom must expand his or her awareness, to come out of the darkness of negativity.

Thoth advised that those who want to follow the ways of wisdom, the Pathways to Light, must open their minds to the beauty of life and nature. They must expand their consciousness and bring it out of Darkness, to allow it to flow freely through all time and space.

Meditation for an Out-of-Body Experience

Thoth was advocating meditation and outlined his own way of releasing his soul from its physical prison. Before starting any form of meditation there needs to be some preparation though. The body will need to be free of heavy foods, especially any form of meat, all of which contains the fear of the animal it was taken from. All negative energy binds the soul to the physical body, preventing an out-of-body experience.

It is helpful to begin with a short prayer, asking for the Light to be with you and freeing you from whatever heavy emotions might prevent you from becoming free of the Dark, to escape beyond the veil and into the greater Worlds of Light. Once you have prepared your body and freed it of all stresses, lie down in a darkened quiet place to protect your mind from any sudden disturbances.

- Relax and go into a deep silence.
- Free yourself from all thoughts of desire, knowing that you are already one with all.
- Silence any thoughts which arise in your mind.
- Bring your consciousness, your thoughts, to the centre of your mind, then shake it free from its

place in the Dark by visualising rising spirals that will lift you out of your body.
- Move up through the spiral, which holds the soul to the body.
- Do this with force until you are free and out of your body.
- Then let your mind take you to what you seek to know, and see the mysteries for yourself.

At the end of the meditation, when you are returning to your body, it is important to feel yourself spiralling back in. Your personal spiral is like an ethereal fingerprint that only you can use. This way you protect your body from being invaded by alien energies.

Prayer for Ascension

The power of the cosmos rests in harmony and balance; everything moves in order to the harmony of music and colour. This is an energy far beyond mankind, who lives in his fears and desires. You can only become one with the consciousness of the planes above when you have come out of the darkness of negative thought. Once free of negative emotion, a power will flow through you which is the light of your soul.

Thoth offers a prayer to help you find the light and wisdom of your soul.

Mighty Spirit of Light.
That shines through the universe.
Draw my soul closer to you.
Lift up my thoughts from out of the Darkness.
Most powerful Lord, who gives to us all.
Lift up my soul, oh Lord of the Light.
Draw me to your power,
that I become one with your Light.
Lord of all things, and all things to come.
Power of my life-force,
and one with my thoughts.
Bless me with Light,
which is the force of my life.

Once you have freed your soul from the bondages of negativity, you will be free to live in the creative worlds of imagination and contentment. You will have found the Keys of Wisdom.

So far, Thoth had identified two of the Three Keys of Wisdom.

- ♀ Freedom from fear, a peace that transcends all peace
- ♀ Freedom from all thoughts of desire, knowing that you are already one with everything that is

… Now he must search for the third essential Key.

THE LOST PLANE OF ATLANTIS

THOTH OFTEN DREAMED OF the Earth when it was still part of the Atlantean Continent. He thought of that once beautiful paradise in which he grew up, and remembered the vibrant life that once inhabited it. A world filled with light that shone through the darkness of night, but which now lay separate from the beauty and safety of Great Atlantis, beneath the darkness of negative energy.

He remembered when the Earth Plane was still governed by earth-born masters, such as his father, who had the support and wisdom of the Lords who acted as one, to hold the planes in balance, one with the other.

The Lord of All, known but unknown, moved without moving through all the planes that held the continent of Atlantis in balance. Far advanced beyond the comprehension of mankind, he lived in the planes with no need for a body. Using his power, he came down amongst men, seen but unseen, heard but unheard.

This Lord of Light was never one with the people born to Earth. He was the one who held the Keys of

Wisdom, who guided mankind in the Ways of the Light. He showed the people the Pathways to Light, the way to ascend from one plane to the next. He showed the way out of Darkness, leading the soul up through the planes to ever more beautiful creations.

It was the Lord of Light, the creator and Lord of all things, who divided the continent into ten different planes, to be inhabited by the Children of Light. These children are beyond mankind, they have separated themselves from the Dark.

On each of the ten planes the Lord built a Temple of Light, a gateway or connection point, through which his power would flow from the highest to the lowest, and back. He built one of these temples on each plane, using the power of his awareness, forces of imagination unknown to mankind.

From the energy of space the Great Lord created the continent of Atlantis, whose planes rose one above the other, in the shape of a pyramid. Only a totally positive spirit with high awareness and creative imagination can create something from nothing, and fill the nothing with beauty and greatness.

Three Masters were chosen to convey his thoughts through the Worlds of Atlantis, and a further Seven Masters to rule over the souls of men, with the intention to raise humanity away from the Dark Path to become one with the radiant beauty of the light.

These were the same Masters who were responsible

for keeping the balance between the planes and bore the titles of Lords, not yet including the two Masters who would become responsible for the Underworlds.

As Thoth tells us, he only ever sought wisdom and though wrapped in Darkness, he never stopped searching for the elusive light. He tells us of his travels along the Pathway to Light, pursuing nothing but more and more knowledge.

For many centuries, Thoth had been searching for knowledge and wisdom, when one of the Three Masters brought him to the Great Temple and into the presence of the Lord of Light. The Lord was seated on a great throne, clothed in a light that was flashing with power, and which washed through and over Thoth in waves of brightness.

In his soul, Thoth heard the voice of the Great Lord, inviting him to come out of his searching and into the Light. The voice continued to explain that he had been noticed for his persistence, and that every soul who struggles to be free of the Cycle of Rebirth will succeed, if they follow the laws of the universe as Thoth had done.

Thoth was invited to stay with the Masters and learn all they could teach him. An opportunity he would follow to fulfil his dream and become one of the Masters, holding the Power of the Light. For this, he was told, he would be free of the Lord of Life and Death, and would no longer have to live through the Darkness known to mankind.

The Great Lord continued, telling Thoth that he would now live through the ages and be free of the Cycle of Rebirth, to record the wisdom which he was bound to learn from the Masters. That he was to keep himself ready for the time when the Power of the Light would wash over the Earth in big waves, to separate it from the main body of Atlantis.

Until then, Thoth was to live in the highest of the temples, the Great Temple, free to learn all that there was to know until he was filled with the Awareness of Light. He was also able to use the gateways that led deep into the Halls of Amenti, where the awareness of nature in all its shapes and forms is stored. Where he would yet learn more of the laws that balance the worlds.

Using his power in accordance with the law, Thoth was able to penetrate the hidden spirals of energy that maintain the balance of the Earth. He was able to see into the energy of the future as easily as he could see into the energy of the past. He learned how to read the thoughts in the hearts of men, how to know their pasts and the futures they had caused for themselves.

He was shown how everyone shapes their own destiny by the choices they make and the way they have lived in the past. It is not the Lord of Light who makes problems for mankind, but mankind itself by craving to gather or destroy that for which they have no use.

Thoth saw that Atlantis was not only surrounded by

light-energy but also by dark-energy. He wanted to know what this darkness was, but was warned that it is forbidden to search for the pathways that lead to the Dark. It was explained to him that there were some who had risen to the heights of known knowledge, and who had become overproud of what they knew, thinking themselves better and superior to others. This had caused them to fall into the Ways of Darkness.

It had been these same people who had opened up pathways for the Dark to come through, something forbidden by spiritual law. Although they had also been seeking knowledge, the knowledge they were seeking was of the dark-energy, with which they intended to imprison and control the minds and souls of other men. They were searching in the Dark to bring to the surface the Ways of Darkness, wanting to dominate and control the plane of Lower Atlantis for their own purposes of superiority and power.

Anyone who searches in the Dark must have balance and be stronger than that which they wish to dominate. Otherwise they will be drawn to its depths and become lost prisoners of the Dark, unable to find their way back to the Light. These fallen men, in their arrogance and superiority, became prisoners to the Laws of Darkness and were unable to escape.

But in his place, in the highest plane of Atlantis, the Great Lord had seen what was happening below. He saw that the Atlanteans on Earth had opened a gateway into the dark-energy, which was allowing negative energy to enter their world, bringing great harm to the whole of Atlantis.

He called the Three Masters to his Temple of Light and instructed them to shatter the pathway that connects the Earth with the Worlds of Atlantis. He also called upon the Seven Masters and told them to use their powers to change the balance of the Earth Plane, so that it would be separated from the ethereal energy that runs through the higher planes.

Once this was done, great waves of energy swept over the Earth, causing the oceans to rage over the lands, destroying everything along the way.

As a result, the gateway that had existed for eons was shattered and lost by a change in the balance. At this point it was left to Thoth and the Seven Masters to instruct those who were born to the Earth, on how to use their positive energy of awareness and creative imagination to find their way back to the ethereal continent of Atlantis.

There will always be teachers to instruct those who search for the path that leads to paradise, but only those who follow the laws will be able to find their way back.

Thoth had now found the final Key of Wisdom that would bring humanity out of Darkness, making it a total of three.

- ♀ Freedom from fear: to know a peace that transcends all peace
- ♀ Freedom from desire: to know you already have all you need
- ♀ Freedom from superiority: an energy that leads only to Darkness

The Astral World

When it was finished and the negative energy had been cleared from the face of the Earth, the innocence of vegetation and other forms of nature re-established themselves, and the early stages of humanity began to evolve.

The Great Lord was now sure that it was time to begin, and instructed Thoth to take his wisdom and knowledge and teach the growing human race in the ways of creative beauty and greatness, so that they would become worthy of returning to Great Atlantis. Thoth was instructed to stay with the people until they had completed a program of lives, which would give them the experience they needed to develop and prepare themselves for the spiritual planes above.

It was to be a cycle of lives, moving between the Earth and ten different Astral Levels, with no less than twelve lives on each level. Beginning with the first and lowest level, and finishing with the tenth and highest level. This would continue until the individual soul had completed the program through all ten levels. When the final level was completed, the soul would have freed itself of all negative attitudes and emotions, and be ready to ascend into the spiritual planes of Atlantis.

Thoth watched as the Masters constructed the Astral World of ten ascending levels of energy, which was a copy of the pyramid of Atlantis. The first and lowest level was only separated from the Earth by a thin veil. But those who had become addicted to the illusion of pleasure were unable to move through this veil, and so were not totally separated from their addictions.

The full force of negative emotion would be felt by those in this in-between state, who craved for what they had lost – close enough to touch, but not to have. These souls are too spiritually asleep to see what harm they are doing to themselves. They have become so addicted to desire and pleasure that they do not wake up from their sleep-state in the After Life and are quickly reborn back into the addictions of life, which they have mistaken for pleasure.

It is people who are born from this level between the Earth and the Astral World, who sometimes experience an association with a past life because they have not completely disconnected from the emotions of their previous time on Earth, and so they relive all the old emotions in their new life. This can be especially awkward for people who are born into the opposite gender from the one in their past, because although the body has changed, the emotions will have stayed the same.

The space between the Earth and the First Astral Level is a lawless world, close to the Underworld and full of emotional temptations. This is also the level where disconnected emotional bodies such as thought forms and other disembodied energies exist.

Once past the thin veil, the soul would either return to the same Astral Level, or the next higher one, depending on how well it has done. Anyone who has deliberately caused hurt to others, through any form of perversion, or who has caused chaos and destruction during their lives and not atoned for it in form of suffering while alive, will be drawn down into one of the Underworlds.

From here it is an existence of struggle to rise back to any form of peace and beauty. But those who have their emotions under better control and who have struggled to fight against the many temptations, will arrive in the first level of the Astral World, or even higher if they have lived an unselfish life.

Only those who honour nature and live unselfishly, helping others to do the same, will find their way into one of the higher Astral Levels. Here, on the other side of the veil, the soul is fully awake and can review in depth the life it has just experienced.

Then again, time in the Astral World is none of blissful leisure. It is one of instruction, with a spiritual guide to help and direct the souls who are willing to listen, so that in the next life they can benefit from the experiences of the previous ones.

Here in the After Life, the soul will review and witness the physical life it has just completed, and prepare to use the experience for the next life on Earth, where the soul will be expected to correct any hurt it has caused, or mistakes it has made.

There are some who feel overwhelmed by guilt as they watch the results of what they have said or done. But wrongs committed on Earth cannot be corrected in the Astral World and have to be put right in a future life.

Being reborn from one of the lower Astral Levels usually means returning to the same family situation as the one they have left, especially if they have unfinished business or karma to work through.

The biggest hurdle for mankind to overcome is the first level, which is closest to the Earth. Any attachments or desires that have not been overcome will pull the soul back into physical life, without having learned anything. Some souls go around and around the Cycle of Life and Death on the same level for hundreds of lives without evolving.

It helps to know that in coming to the After Life one will never be alone, and that anyone who has experienced great trauma or horror in their dying moments will first arrive in a place of peace and calm, where they can recover before moving on to their appropriate level.

And of course, there will always be people waiting for you in the After Life, whom you have known and loved, or been attached to in other ways, but only as long as it is your wish to meet with them again.

After time spent in the Astral World, souls would return to Earth to be reborn and begin another life, which will hold the lessons they need to experience. Only by rejecting the Dark Path and learning how to control the emotional personality, which is placed on everyone at birth to strengthen their resolve against temptation, can anyone earn their rightful place to return to the Paradise of Atlantis. Only in this way can someone overcome the recurring Cycle of Birth and Death with its emotional difficulties of life on Earth.

Everyone has to pass through all Ten Astral Levels to free themselves of the negative energies they might have unknowingly brought with them from Earth. Like a cleansing process.

Sphinx and Pyramid

When the construction of the Astral World was finished, Thoth and 32 Masters from the higher Planes of Atlantis travelled along spirals, through the energies that separate the Planes of Atlantis from the Astral Levels, and onto the Earth.

They travelled in a translucent bubble of positive energy, which they later buried deep beneath the rocks, and where they erected a marker in the form of what we later would come to name the *Sphinx*. This image has the face of an Atlantean and the body of a lion, a symbol of *controlled power*.

Thoth writes in his records that far into the future, the human race will be invaded by Dark Forces, and when this happens, the positive energy which had been buried under the Sphinx will be released to overpower the dark and negative force. This dark emotional energy will come from the Underworlds, through those who are living and following the Path of Darkness, causing chaos in the world.

The Pyramid, Thoth says, he built as a symbol that leads to Atlantis. But all of Thoth's writings and constructions are symbolic and not easily deciphered. He tells us that only those searching for Truth will understand the deeper meanings of the symbols and hidden messages in his work.

So, into seen and unseen spaces within the pyramid, Thoth left information and instructions transcribed as energy. As it stands, the pyramid is a symbol of the mind, illustrating the power of positive energy and creative imagination. The power of the mind, as in the pyramid, flows up from the base to the apex, in the fashion of a spiral.

At the point of the apex the power is at its most intense and where the soul finds its freedom. The way for a soul to escape from the darkness of life is to travel along such spirals of awareness. But to enter the higher spheres through the window of your mind, it is necessary to remember the Three Keys of Wisdom.

- ♀ Freedom from Fear
- ♀ Freedom from Desire
- ♀ Freedom from Superiority

ASCENSION

THOTH TRAVELLED DEEP into the energy that separates the Earth from Atlantis. He travelled into the energy of emotion, the Astral World, and found there were deep hidden pathways there that, though known, are unseen by the hearts of men.

He searched for the wisdom in the hearts and souls of men, and realised it was hidden behind the Darkness in their lives. He saw that humanity was living in Darkness and through the energy of emotion that blocks the Power of Light, preventing people from being as free as they were expected to be.

Under the direction of the Great Lord there are the Seven Masters who rule over the souls of men, and are responsible for maintaining the balance of the Seven Spiritual Planes. These spiritual planes are mirrored within all human life, under the law of *'as above, so below'*. If you allow yourself to follow spiritual law, you become a perfect representation of Atlantis.

Below the continent there is the isolated Earth Plane, onto which you were born, and below that are the two dark realms of the Underworld, which came into existence because of the negativity and the destructive thoughts of mankind that caused the flood.

The souls who exist in these Dark Worlds wander around lost until they begin to find goodness in their way of thinking. At this point, they begin the journey back to the Light, but it is a long and weary struggle that they face, having fallen so low into the Dark.

Two Masters are intrusted to guard these Underworlds, and then there are the Seven Masters, the Chakra Masters, who control the laws and lessons of ascension while you are in the program of the Cycle of Lives.

During the time you spend moving from the lowest to the highest level of the Astral World, you will have spiritual guides leading you through the various lessons. This is not someone you will be aware of while you are incarnated on Earth, but someone you will be very aware of in the periods between your lives.

Spiritual guides follow your progress and are responsible for helping you ascend the several stages of the journey through the Astral World, as you struggle to overcome the many negative temptations. These guides and many other helpers are constantly with you through this difficult part of the ascending process, as you progress in tiny steps through the different levels.

The body is your personal temple for the time you are living on Earth. This temple is connected to the Astral Levels through a system of connectors that Thoth refers to as *Flowers,* and which are watched over by the Seven

Chakra Masters. This is because in appearance every one of these connection points do look very much like a flower that protrudes from the body on a long stalk. They are more commonly known by their Indian names as *Chakras*.

Each of the Chakras has a different number of petals, with the one at the base having the least and the one at the top the most. Every petal represents a different part of your character, depending on the placement of the Chakra in the body. To most people the Chakras are invisible, and only those who have an exceptionally high energy will be able to see them.

These connections to the Astral Levels and their Masters, through the Flower System, are set to guide you through the lessons of life which were agreed upon before you were born. They can only be changed by the thoughts of the Seven Masters or by yourself, which happens when you change or adjust your attitude towards life.

No one else can interfere, manipulate, or intervene with your Chakras in any shape or form because if they could, your life would end in disaster.

The purpose of the Flower System is to steer you into and through the various and ever-changing complications of life. This includes thought patterns such as enthusiasm, purpose, health, happiness, determination, instinct and a whole host of attitudes, too many to mention.

The problems, as you have already seen, are the independent emotions which have no association with the spiritual world, the World of Atlantis. Emotions will be constantly trying to dominate your thinking with their own selfish needs, turning you away from your spiritual path, or encouraging you to do or say things which in your heart you know are not right.

The more spiritually asleep you are, the more the emotions will determine your life, ignoring the Ways of the Masters.

It is through these *Flowe*rs that the Seven Masters connect with you, and they are arranged vertically through your body.

The lower three are located in the areas of the base of the spine, the spleen, and the solar plexus. These guide you through the first 23 years of life, when you are learning about and concerned with things such as survival, pleasure, self-worth, career choices, sex, confidence and independence. This is a critical time in your life because if you are unable to control your emotions, they will lead you into all sorts of problems and away from the advice and guidance of the Masters.

It is a time in life when an experienced soul will avoid any association with the negative aspects of survival and pleasure, whereas people in the first three stages of the astral climb would lose their way without the help of the Masters. This is a time when the forces of your own emotions, and those of others around you, seem to be trying to resist your independence and common sense. Always remember that we were not born to be a slave to the expectations of other people.

The next two Chakras in the Flower System connect you with a concern for other people and their well-being, and the interest you had in your own survival and personal needs becomes much less than it was in the first 23 years of your life.

These two Chakras are located around the heart and throat areas, and the influence of the two responsible Masters becomes more active and increasingly significant from around 23 years of age. This period will last until you are about 42. It is during the middle years of your life when you will be incredibly open to reacting to other people's emotions.

At some point during this time, the Master responsible will start to divert the energy, which enters through your heart, from the lower part of your Flower System to the higher placed Chakras. This causes you to feel less concerned about survival and pleasure, and more concerned about the higher reasons for life and purposes.

Clearly, the amount of influence these two Masters have on your life is very much dependent on your ability to control your emotions. The more advanced souls will feel the influence of these two Masters over a much longer period of their lives than the less experienced ones.

People of the first three stages of the astral climb will feel a strong emotional pull towards the lower Chakras in the Flower System for most of their lives, whereas more advanced souls will start to direct their energy to the higher Chakras at an earlier age. Naturally, this does not include those whose only reason for caring is for what they can gain out of it, as such people are still working through the lower Chakras of selfishness. It all very much depends on how far up the astral ladder you have progressed, on how in-control of your emotions you are, and what sort of lessons you were born into.

In the final stages of your life, any time after the age of 42, the two *Flowers* located in the areas of the brow and the top of the head start to open, and dominate your thinking and decision making until the end of life.

This later period of life is about developing intuition, awareness, philosophy, healing, wisdom, etc., especially for those who are in the final stages of the Astral Ascension. A stage when you begin to think about your connection and relationship with the Light.

Others on the other hand, still have many lifetimes to go through before their last two Chakras become activated.

Your success in any of these pursuits is again very much dependent on where you are in your astral climb. If you have only just entered the sixth level for example, your interest in connecting with the Light will be slight, but if you are nearing the end of the Cycle of Rebirth, your interests will be very much in knowing about the spiritual worlds. However, you will not be very interested in the limiting aspects of religious philosophy which tends to concern you in earlier stages.

The speed at which you ascend through the Astral Levels very much depends on how well you have succeeded in limiting the emotional and negative attitudes in your lives.[5]

What Thoth is doing through his records is giving people reasons and explanations for the struggles, difficulties and disappointments in their lives. There are no easy lessons and your lives, which could be hundreds if you are a slow learner, will involve the whole range of emotions.

You will need to learn how to manage problems such as devastating loss, loneliness, poverty, health problems, depression and so on... It is *how* you manage these difficulties that will determine the speed of your ascension. The worst of all reactions would probably be self-pity.

You will also be judged on how you managed your successes. Were you generous, or cruel? Did you help others, or did you steal self-worth from those less fortunate? Did you stay humble, or did you pride yourself in your successes?

We are all following in the thoughts of greater souls,

---

[5] If you wish to read more about the Mechanics of a Chakra, please refer to Part Four in my earlier book 'Where the Soul Flies'.

who came before us and have struggled no less than ourselves, before reaching their goal of self-perfection and freedom from the Lord of Life and Death. Everything moves in spirals, and those who are prepared to struggle to be free of the Cycle of Rebirth will be lifted on the spiral of positive energy that eventually leads back to Atlantis.

You will come through the Astral Levels faster, if you always search for contentment in what you have. Always keep high in your thoughts the need to avoid unnecessary fear, doubt or worry, to be aware of desire when there is no need, and the dangers of superiority in times of success. Unfortunately, it is much easier to fall through the spirals than it is to rise if you become distracted by pleasure or material dreams.

The Seven Masters who connect you with the Astral World work according to spiritual law, and these laws cannot be changed to suit one's inclinations. If you go against the pull of life, against what you know to be true, life will be a struggle and end in tears of disappointment.

The Flower System is arranged to determine and guide your destiny, to bring you closer to the end of your rebirths.

Every spiritual guide is there to help you through to the next level, and you need to follow where the Masters lead. Even if you feel your emotions pulling you in the opposite direction, do not give in to them. There is a guide to help and direct you on every step of the way, and if you ask and listen in the quiet of your thoughts you will hear the answers.

It is so extremely easy to be caught in the web of emotion, which is one of the main barriers to advancing away from the Wheel of Reincarnation. Learning to understand how emotions interfere with your destiny will help you to stay clear of the Dark.

The Seven Masters

Thoth tells us that there are Seven Masters of knowledge and wisdom, but they do not exist in a fixed form as we understand it. They have no shape that can be understood or seen. They are an energy of wisdom, born out of an awareness with creative imagination. An awareness that understands your need to be, and to become one with it.

Their energy is too powerful and overwhelming for them to become one with human life. When they communicate, it is not as a separate personality that your senses can see, feel, or hear. Instead, you are being absorbed into their thoughts, pulled into their energy to hear their wisdom.

Once you become one with them, you change to know what they know, and to feel what they feel.

It was explained to Thoth that to change anything for the better, he would need to take it into his heart and mind, just as he himself was being taken into the hearts and minds of the Masters of Wisdom to know what they knew. It is not possible to cause change by going *to* something.

'*If someone asks for help, bring that person into your heart, so that he or she can benefit from your knowledge, wisdom and balance,*' he was told.

Only in this way could he perform change in the energy of anyone or anything.

If he was to allow himself to go into the energy of someone else's situation he would become the smaller one, and he would be the one to be changed, for better or worse.

'*Because when you bring a person or situation into your own heart and mind you are the dominant one, the terminating factor. And provided you are free of emotion and open to acceptance of everything without judgement, whatever or whoever is seeking your help will change to be the image of your positive thoughts.*

'*You cannot change a situation by becoming one with it. In this position you are always the weaker force, and you won't be able to be the necessary force for change. To change something you need to bring the situation, whatever it is, into yourself.*

'*Change comes when you are master of the situation, and this you can only do by bringing the situation into your own energy, without fear, desire, or superiority. All life will lie at your feet in surrender if you offer yourself as its sanctuary, where there is no judgement. But, no life or situation will surrender itself to you if you are driven by emotion. No situation will trust any thoughts that would desert, use, or dominate.'*

The only way to help someone is to bring the problem into one's peace and calm, so that the person in need can adapt to be as well as the strong and healthy. But, if ruled by emotion this will work against the one helping because there is no trust in a situation ruled by emotion.

Emotion is unreliable and can change in an instant. Emotion is a tool of the Dark, to encourage with offerings and easy talk. Once you are in its web, it will twist and turn until you are wrapped in its silky threads of deceit, unable to escape without hurt or damage to your soul.

When emotion uses guilt as a weapon, it is at its most dangerous because it becomes the victim and the enemy at the same time, taking away any form of defence.

Unless you have your emotions on a strong leash, so that they walk behind you and not in front, Darkness can easily become your master.

With the highest Masters of Atlantis to guide him, Thoth learned the secrets of time and space. He had no words to express the greatness, or the wisdom which was being unfolded for him to explore.

He was shown how to access both the future and the past by attracting it to himself, instead of going to it.

Both, the past and the future, will come to you when they know what you want – although fear, desire or superiority will act as a barrier.

Thoth was also told that people learn by absorbing the energy of knowledge; only in this way can they use knowledge to give it life as wisdom. Knowledge learned by pure study is soon forgotten, and not carried forward from life to life. Logic has a short life, while knowledge absorbed through the energy of experience and reasoning becomes part of you, through to eternity's end.

This is how the Masters control their energy, they bring into themselves whatever it is they want to know or need to change.

The Seven Masters have no need to be seen. You sense their presence, they are already with you, one with every level of your thinking. At their level of awareness they don't need to be physical. It is the power of your own positive awareness, and the acceptance of knowledge greater than your own that allows them to guide you.

If you trust your thoughts they will enclose your soul in an intelligent mist, so that you become one with their wisdom. This is how they share their awareness. The Masters would never demand or force obedience, they offer you to surrender to their knowledge and wisdom, so they can guide you as need be.

Through the minds of the Seven Masters you can know things you could not possibly have known with your own insignificant library of thoughts.

When knowledge comes to your mind, which you know you could not previously have known or understood, you have entered into a greater library. This is where the positive energy of imagination is being used by the Masters, and what you learn while you are in the halls of this great library will thus become part of your own awareness.

Imagination is the search engine of the mind.

It was Thoth's positive imagination and awareness that allowed him to grow in wisdom. There is nothing in the mind of man that was not originally in the thoughts of the Seven Masters. These great beings exist in a space without time or substance.

This does not mean that they are without personality. Each of them has a defined personality that is unique to itself, and you can call on them for help at any time once you become aware of them. To know them is to have access to the Universal Library of unlimited knowledge and wisdom. There is not a question you could ask that has not already been answered in one of these seven incredible minds.

But the libraries are kept locked from negative thought, as negative thought would destroy the information and wisdom within, which is held for the benefit of the souls searching for the Light.

The Sphinx, as a symbol, has more than one meaning and this is a further one.

It is a clear mind that connects to the higher spheres, not the emotion.

They are the same Seven Masters who will put questions and difficulties into your life, problems for you to solve. Overcoming these problems of life will strengthen your awareness and imagination.

These Masters teach through difficulties, so that life seems to be a struggle. They know your past and your weaknesses, and highlight them in your life to make you aware and stronger. There are no easy lessons for those on the Path to the Light.

These Seven Masters of Wisdom are not known by name. How can you name an energy that has no form, no permanent place, and exists everywhere but nowhere?

They come from the future and know everything of the past. They live forever but have no identity, they are free from death but have no life. They are awareness without form, they are imagination without image. They are the everything in nothing, and the nothing in everything. Yet still, they exist.

Joined as one with the other Great Masters, they are the total of all. As one, they are the Master of All, the greatest of all, but also the smallest of all. This great omnipresence is always with you, but you never know of it because of its smallness.

Thoth tells us that the Great Lord is both the largest and the smallest at the same time. When you put the largest cell in the human body, the ovum or the egg cell of a female, together with the smallest cell in the human body, the sperm cell of a male, you have life – you have awareness.

Only when you accept that life comes from both the largest and the smallest, separate but joining to become one, will you understand that all is in one, and one is in all. Once you comprehend this you will understand how the Seven Masters, the Chakra Masters, work separately though united, to lead humanity through to the Light.

As astonishing as it sounds, Thoth was talking about genetics and awareness thousands of years ago. He was explaining how awareness and imagination work together, but remain separate and free of negativity.

It's difficult to grasp the vastness of what Thoth was introducing to the new developing form of humanity.

In the Light

The Great Masters explained to Thoth that although they were as men they were unlike men, since they had no need of a personal identity. This was only possible because they had given up their ego, their need to be different, to be seen or recognised. It is the ego, which keeps mankind from becoming one with the soul of creative awareness.

Thoth was told that he needed to stop thinking of himself as a separate identity. Emotions will always have a need to be noticed, as someone different and special. Strength and knowledge become stronger when you overcome the emotions, which have a need to be seen as someone separate or superior.

'Learn to value all life as equal and one with your own awareness, including nature. It is when you can combine your thoughts with all other levels of awareness that true strength and wisdom becomes available,' Thoth was told.

The Seven Masters explained that they were speaking from the Soul of Nature, which is where all awareness originates. So, why would they want to be separate from it? The Masters are one with the knowledge of their planes, and all that they hold. This, Thoth was told, is wisdom. Wisdom to become one with the Natural World, on which everything relies for its awareness.

'You must think as nature thinks,' they insisted.

'A tree is a tree and enjoys just being a tree. It goes nowhere, does nothing, just enjoys being a tree. It has no thoughts about how it looks or how others value it. It just enjoys being a tree. It is the people who give the tree its beauty, and make it special with their thoughts. But the tree is not concerned with how others feel about it, it just enjoys being a tree. It does not worry or feel sad if the life it supports in its branches and roots leaves, to find

shelter in another tree. It just continues enjoying what it is, a tree.

'Be like the tree, Thoth, and teach how to be free of fear, desire and superiority. Be like the tree, a friend to all forms of life just because you are there, and not because of anything you do or say. It is for others to decide who *or* what *you are.'*

The Seven Masters continued:

'In a time that is not yet a time, all those who seek wisdom shall become one in understanding with the greatest creative awareness of all. This is to know the thoughts and balance of nature, its struggles and its contentment, its past and its headed direction.

'Nature holds the keys to the laws of the universe. Learn these laws,' he was told, *'and they will carry you past the guardians that live at the door to the Light.'*

This, Thoth realised, was the wisdom he had been searching for.

Next spoke the Three Masters:

'We have existed beyond a time known to man, tasting neither life nor death. And know this, Thoth, that far in a future unknown to man, life and death will become as one. Each so perfectly balanced by the other that neither shall exist.

'Man on the spiral to Light, searching for truth and wisdom, will become one with the Lord of All. For now,

as you see, we have manifested in your time, in the space of now, *but at the same moment we stay in our own time, which is your future time and space. In this highest of the planes time does not exist, and we have no form, nor do we have any separate lives. Even so, our existence is fuller, greater and freer than yours.'*

The Three Masters continued:

'Man is a soul bound to the truth, and although you cannot yet be one with the total truth, you can never be free of the truth.

'When you have progressed through the spirals that lift you from life to life, and entered into the higher planes of Atlantis, life as you understand it will cease to be. Only the essence of your soul and its light, as truth, will remain.

'All that you know is a part of the smallest part. You have not yet touched on the greater part of the truth and its wisdom.

'When you rise to the Light you will be beyond life and death. But first, you must go through the Astral Barriers and the struggles that will loosen you from the body, which holds you to life and death.

'Tell those who wish to know, to look for the path that takes them beyond earthly life. It is not possible to leave the physical shell while still living with emotion. They need to move into a consciousness above the one they know. There is no emotional barrier that cannot be overcome, and once they have succeeded they will be

wearing a body that is the image of their thoughts. Then, and only then, will they be free of the Dark Path that holds them from the Light and the Truth.'

And so, through the ages Thoth listened and learned, knowing that the way to the Heights of Atlantis was through the lessons and struggles of life.

Now, as he nears the end of his journey, Thoth knows that he is shining with Light, with no need of an image. He knows that he has to shatter the Darkness of Ego which still holds close, and let it fall into the Light. And as he comes out of his Darkness, he gives this advice.

'Everyone can be free and live in the Brightness of the Light. Keep your face turned towards the light of integrity, and your soul will live in its brightness. Because you are a Child of the Light.'

And he also adds a warning:

'Don't let your thoughts turn back towards the Dark, hiding the brightness of contentment that flows through your soul. Do not turn to the Dark-Brightness, which is the illusion of pleasure because this comes from the Brothers of the Dark. Keep your eyes always in tune with your soul, and the Light.

'Listen to the wisdom I give you. Listen to the voice in your soul. This is the Path to Brightness, the way to be one with the Light and the Truth.'

As we have been shown, there is no death in the spiritual planes. There, life does not stop and start as it does on Earth. When the time comes for a spirit to ascend to the next Plane of Atlantis, it will not be because of a tired or sick body. There are no health problems on the planes above the Earth. Only when the soul has freed itself of all negative emotion is it allowed to enter into the higher levels of awareness.

Ascending through the Planes of Atlantis does not happen in the same way as it does in the Astral Levels. When you have finished the Rebirth Program successfully, the spirit ascends quietly and without death into the next plane.

After eons, too long to assess, the spirit will have grown in knowledge and wisdom, to become a light of creative awareness that surpasses the world it is in. It is then that the spirit will feel a need to enter into a place of total peace and contentment. A place which will be filled with all form of nature's beauty.

This space is pure beyond anything the spirit will so far have experienced, with the colours of a hue that is not found anywhere in the lower worlds. There is no heaviness in this place, everything floats across the ground so that nothing is disturbed or damaged.

The spirit will not be alone in this magnificent place. There will be many who have come together in anticipation of an important event. People clothed in robes of pastel shades will be sitting above the grass, either alone or in groups. They will have been attracted to this beautiful valley by some inner power.

Everything: the grass, the flowers, the trees, the brook as it meanders its way through the valley, everything is alive with an awareness of contentment and happiness, as if welcoming you into their world.

Animals of the forest and the meadows wander amongst these spirits, totally in harmony with their surroundings and with no fear or distrust. Birds seem to be hanging in the air on the strings of their beautiful melodious notes.

All around is peace and contentment, which nothing can disturb. No earth-bound soul could explain in words the beauty and harmony that is found in this Valley of Atlantis. There will be an air of expectancy in the atmosphere, but also one of absolute peace and contentment.

Then, from some distant place, the gathered spirits will hear the sound of music, a choir of angels. As the sound approaches, the colours over the ground and in the air change to radiate a subtle energy of illumination. And at last, the distant choir of angels will be on every side of this special place. All around the angels fill the air with their enchanted music which is beautiful beyond anything that is possible to describe.

After a while, the choir divides to fill either side of this heavenly space, until a vision of the Great Lord appears. The brilliance of the Lord's energy shines into every part of the valley, so that no one can ignore it. It is the energy of absolute serenity. With that, an energy of pink mist begins to enter the space and drift amongst the enchanted spirits.

This mist will have an exotic smell of roses, and many other perfumed flowers. Some will be touched by this pink mist, which changes their robes to be of the same colour. Those who are touched by this spiritual energy will rise unaided, to float into the air and through the choir of angels. When the last of those who have been touched by the perfumed pink fragrance have ascended, the Lord withdraws, followed by the choir of angels until all is peaceful and calm again.

Those who are left will know that they have witnessed a great spiritual event. They will feel empowered to continue with their own work, learning the laws of awareness and creativity to grow in knowledge and wisdom. So that perhaps next time, they also will be touched by the Light of the Lord.

There is no death or reincarnation on the Planes of Atlantis. Those who ascend have no need to return unless they wish to.

There is no loss of consciousness in moving from one plane to the next. And there is no mourning or grieving for those who have moved on. Such negative emotions have long been left behind, in the worlds below the Planes of Atlantis.

MYSTERIES

NOW THAT THOTH HAD BECOME a Master of Men, he was eager to pass on the wisdom he had learned. He wants you to know what he experienced during his travels through space above and beyond the Planes of Atlantis.

As he explains, he is no longer a man in the way mortals would expect him to be, he is no longer tied to a physical or emotional body. He is able to travel from place to place, and he can change his appearance to suit whatever situation he finds himself in.

He tells us about the wonders of the Great Masters, who guard and protect the planes and dimensions that hold everything in balance.

'There are no mysteries,' he tells us. *'There is only hidden knowledge, waiting to be found. Find the hidden knowledge and you will master the Darkness to be one with the Light. Knowledge is all around, but hidden deep.'*

He implores you to keep going and overcome the Realms of Darkness, which are the emotions that would hold you back.

The world is changing and humanity is changing with it, and because the human soul is not of this world it must move on. It must let go of everything emotion is using as an illusion, blinding you to the reality of awareness, and causing you to feel safe and comfortable.

The people of the Earth have been caught in a web of emotion to prevent the soul from leaving its mortal prison. If you want to become one with the Light, and move out of the cycle of rebirth and into the planes above, it will mean giving up your body, your identity, your ego, your attachments, and everything else you hold dear and important in your physical life. Only when you have done this and left behind the world of identity with its emotions, will you be free to enter the Paradise of Atlantis.

Thoth is insistent that we can all move away from the cycle of rebirth and be one with the Light. But first we must release everything, every emotion that holds us to this material world. You cannot take what you have of this world and this life, with you into the next world. This is one of the mysteries.

Hold nothing, become nothing, and then you become more.

Understand that awareness is your soul, and as the soul you are not a *thing*. Your soul is not a solid substance, it is a free-flowing energy of creative awareness that can expand or reduce itself to suit the situation. The more the soul allows itself to be one with all other positive energy, the more the soul grows.

You are what you know and what you think, you are not the body or the emotions of the mind. You are your soul. It is the negative effects of being emotionally physical that keeps you to the restricted state of rebirth, unaware of your true potential.

The time between lives teaches us how to become free of the limiting effects of negative emotion. If you are prepared to let go of all the illusions in your life, the Astral World will teach you how to become one with all that is, and how to use creative imagination to expand your awareness.

As a soul, you are an energy that exists through all time and space, whichever plane you find yourself in. The essence of your soul is unseen and unfelt by you, but acknowledged by others. Either as a positive imaginative bright light, or an emotionally negative earth-bound personality.

It is knowing who you are and being one with all other energy that prevents you from hurting others or being destructive. Knowing that if you deliberately hurt another, you are hurting yourself at a deeper soul level. You might not feel what the other feels at the time you inflict the hurt, but at a spiritual level your soul will be suffering in torment for not being able to control the emotion meant to cause someone else to suffer. It is not possible to hurt another without first destroying your own imaginative awareness, which would have prevented any form of destruction.

In the higher states of awareness, you will realise that all suffering is an emotional experience. There is no suffering when you are free of the emotions that hold you to rebirth. Only your own dark energy would smother the light of your soul, so that your emotions become free to cause hurt to another. This is another of the mysteries.

To cause hurt, you must first destroy the light you are to be free to hurt.

Thoth tells us that long ago, when the Earth was still directly connected to Atlantis, mankind entered into the darkness of the Underworld to have the power of negative forces for themselves. But, the forces they released into the world were too strong to be controlled.

These destructive forces have no bodies of their own and need to express themselves through the negative energy of emotion, which they find in people. The Dark Forces, which are able to hide in the emotions of mankind, caused people to want more than was good for their souls. So they began taking from others in greed or need to feel superior. This was the beginning of fear and destruction.

The Masters at that time were able to rid the world of the worst of these negative forces, but some remained hidden in space, as shadows. Slowly and over time, the

Dark Forces re-entered the world and became one with the destructive energy in people's character, causing humanity to become a slave of the Dark.

These dark forces can only exist in the emotions of people and through the years, these separate but powerful energies have been establishing themselves across the world. They have crept into positions of power with the intention to overwhelm humanity with negative emotion, and to rule with chaos.

Fear is the main weapon of the Dark, and using the energies of emotion it causes a thirst for more of everything that mankind does not need. Driven mad by desire for more, people become easy to direct in the ways of destruction.

The strongest of these negative forces seeks to control all that it can, and it has learned that arrogance and superiority can be used to control, and to turn man against man. This is another mystery Thoth shares with us.

The Dark Forces can only express themselves through emotion.

Thoth then placed a vision before the world, of what happens to people who follow the Dark Path. He tells us that there are four paths along which man can choose to travel through life.

One path is the path of integrity, which demands honesty and hard work. It is not the easiest path to travel, and there are many obstacles and difficulties along the way, with few advantages to make the journey attractive.

The remaining three paths are those managed by the Dark, and the attraction to these routes are the immediate rewards they offer in wealth, pleasure or power. These paths seem to offer an easy existence, and as the travellers are about to set out on the journey of life they have to make a decision about which of the paths they are going to take.

The travellers are going to need a strong mind to resist all the temptations and bribes offered along the way, if they are going to avoid turning onto one of the Dark Paths.

I. The man who decides to travel along the Path of Power and Superiority, is going to be filled with arrogance and destruction. He will be prepared to trample over anyone who gets in his way as he bullies and demands his way through life, and insists that everyone surrenders their self-respect so that he can add it to his own. This is a short path, and the one who travels this way expects to become rich and famous in recognition and esteem.

II. The Path of Greed is longer than the first one. This man will take more time to travel through life because he does not want to miss any opportunity to amass wealth, even if it means stealing it from others.

Honesty is not a thought that concerns him. He has an overriding need to collect every penny he can, even from those whose need is greater than his own. Wealth has a magnetic power to draw to itself even that which belongs to someone else, which the traveller then spends on trinkets and property for which he has no need. This man shamelessly travels on leaving behind people hungry and broken, without any thought of the hurt or damage he has caused. Eventually he becomes oppressed by fear, fear that the riches he has dishonestly amassed will be taken from him or be lost. He feels that he can trust no one, in the same way that he could not be trusted by anyone.

III. The man who chooses to travel the Path of Pleasure is not concerned with reputation or wealth, so long as he is having a good time. He has no worries about destroying innocence and beauty, or thoughts for the future. This man would never become distressed by the sight of rotting innocence, demolished love, or barren fields of art as he makes his journey through the world of decaying civilization, destroying lives and nature wherever he goes. This is a long journey, and there is much pleasure to occupy the mind as the traveller's thoughts are lulled away from the risks of being infected by the plagues of debauchery, and the diseases of idleness.

IV. There is much to tempt the man, who prefers to live a <u>Life of Integrity</u> in preference to one of power, wealth, or pleasure. It is a long and slow path, and he walks with an awareness of the needs of others, knowing that he will always have enough as he follows to where his soul leads. This is an exhausting journey with few rewards or delights along the way, and he often feels he cannot continue. But, with his heart filled with patience and understanding his faith calls him forward, to guide him to the journey's end.

All paths, no matter where they started or where they lead, finish at the same gate. The keeper of the gate has one condition as he lets the travellers through: that they walk naked onto the Plain of Truth. Covered in nothing but the clothes equal to the thoughts they have gathered on their journey, which will clothe them in the After Life.

The one who lived a life of integrity, helping others where he could, is a wonder to behold. Fully clothed in light and wisdom, to be received with happiness and praise in a paradise of contentment.

This traveller now wears a crown of gold, collected along the Path of Integrity.

The man who lived for pleasure and idleness is now a piteous soul, as he walks through the Gate of Truth, realising what was lost on the reckless path of irresponsibility. His thoughts are going to be a desperate struggle to free himself of the sores and pains that gnaw at his soul, as he struggles to rid himself of the ugliness that drives others from his sight.

This traveller allowed his soul to wither and decay, in the Arena of Pleasure.

Bent under the weight of loss which has replaced his riches and assets, a weak-looking man full of self-pity walks into the After Life, with nothing to clothe him except distress and shame. The Scales of Justice have returned everything, with interest, to those from whom he took, even when their need was greater than his own. Poor and worthless, there is nothing under which to hide this man's empty soul. There is no relief because he had no regard for the glare of justice to come.

This traveller suffocated his soul beneath a desire for Worthless Treasure.

The man who travelled the path of power and arrogance has nothing but the skeleton of his own destruction with which to walk onto the Plain of Truth. Without a shred of humility to offer protection to his self-respect, he is now humbled by the light of awareness of what he has done. A searing pain of regret scars the heart of this distressed phantom of a soul, lost and blind in its own Darkness.

This traveller betrayed his soul for the Illusions of Grandeur and Fame.

Anyone with the power of the light still strong in their soul should search for the wisdom that will bring them out of the cycle of rebirth and free them from the negativity of the Earth Plane. Only then will they be able to escape the energies that plague the world with fear, desire and superiority. Because once you have an addiction or need, the Dark will follow you through the energies of emotion until you are trapped in its web.

Using logic to justify what you are doing will not help because logic, like fear, is a tool of the Dark. Only by travelling in spirals can you escape the Web of the Dark, which would hold you slave and become your master if you give yourself to its service.

Notice how peaceful is the World of Nature, content in what it has and never thirsting for more than is sufficient to satisfy its needs of the day. This is another mystery, which is so deeply hidden that it is visible but not seen.

Don't abandon contentment to have more of what you don't need.

Thoth tells us that we should live quietly in tune with

nature, and trust as nature does that all our needs, but not our wants, will be supplied by the unseen forces of nature.

Do not rely on logical awareness to provide the happiness you seek. Logic is based on negative law, destroying what it does not understand, and avoiding the law of imagination. Logic feeds on the Darkness of Fear. It rarely satisfies your hunger for contentment and peace, and because of its dependency on negativity it becomes the lowest form of communication. It rejects everything that does not fit its own need or reasoning.

Logic is a helpful tool, provided it is always subservient to a positive mind and not allowed to become its master. Logic moves in straight lines, whereas nature, intuition and inspiration move in curves and circles, which allows one to see what logic would miss.

When you search for more than you need the Dark will relentlessly chase you, sensing your energy of greed. Like a hound on the scent of its prey, it is looking to control your soul by luring it away from the protection of the Light, which is to be satisfied with the little you have.

Negative energy creates desire in your thoughts, causing discontentment and fear, and you will only be safe from the Hounds of the Dark when you have escaped the emotion of wanting. You cannot escape the cycle of rebirth with thoughts of want. Such thoughts only attract you back to your desires, again and again, to be reborn into the world of emotion.

Follow the laws which Thoth gives as his wisdom, which is to let go of everything that prevents you from entering the Light and being one with a world where there is no fear.

Thoth repeats many times how necessary it is to follow your heart and not to rely on logic. Your intuition is more reliable because it looks at the longer term state of affairs, even though logic might seem to be the more sensible or desirable approach in the short term.

You can bend and twist any fact to make it sound reasonable, and suit a particular point of view, but this is the way of the Dark and not the Path to the Light.

It is the unheard thoughts of your soul that carry life forward, not the vocal cravings of emotion.

Another trap of the Dark to be wary about is emotional love as an illusion of pleasure, and therefore unreliable. It can disappear in an instant like everything else that is dependent on receiving.

Give of yourself with compassion and empathy, and not for what you can expect when you speak of love. Giving or loving with expectations is always the path of emotion, and it will use every opportunity to entice you into ways that are not for the good of your soul.

At this point, Thoth hands us some further Keys to the Pathway of Wisdom:

- ♀ Release all the illusions that hold you to rebirth
- ♀ Follow the path of integrity
- ♀ Do not abandon contentment to have more of what you do not need
- ♀ Overcome your desire for more
- ♀ Listen to the inner voice of your soul
- ♀ Do not put trust in logic before intuition
- ♀ Hold nothing, become nothing and then you become more
- ♀ Do not let the giving in your heart be an excuse to receive

He is very persistent in his statements about looking beyond this life, and concentrating on real independence in the lives to follow.

As he says, this life is noticeably short if you take the lifespan of the eternal soul into consideration. Physical life is only temporary, and it all comes down to choice. Either to live through the short-term view of negative dependency, knowing this will only result in more of the same, or to concentrate on the long-term view, developing who you are as an independent creative force, which will bring an end to the Cycle of Life and Death and lift you into the Light. The stark choice is to either continue along the Dark Path or travel the Path of Light.

We are repeatedly being told to look to the future and the ways of the Light. You should be working to release your soul from the continuous round of lives to be free to move into the Light, where there is no fear, hurt, illness or feelings of loss. Your strength comes from the power in your soul when it is in harmony with the higher planes of Atlantis.

If you live in the emotion of negativity you cannot experience the full force of life's wonders. If you live a positive life by being a light for others, you will attract more of the same. But you can never reach higher, shine brighter or become more than your darkest thought, which is why it is so important to control all your emotions and not allow them to control you.

You can do all the good it is possible to do, think all the good it is possible to think, but it is your darkest thoughts, your negative and destructive thoughts, which control and determine who you become. As Thoth never tires of reminding us, *'You cannot be master of anything, until you are master of yourself.'*

He ensures us that we are the ultimate of all things and that there is nothing new, only the forgotten. Everything that you could ever be, or the good you have ever been is always within you. All it needs to bring it to life is for you to open your thoughts to the Light, which is already shining in your heart.

'Be a Light, be the strength you are for others to see and feel. Everything you are and can be, everything you

know and the wisdom you search for is already locked into your awareness.'

Thoth tells us that he wasted eons searching for what was already hidden within his soul. All it took to release the full potential of his soul was to *be* the Light, with integrity, which means doing what his heart tells him he needs to do without fear, without desire, and knowing that no soul is either more or less than any other soul.

No one can follow negativity except by becoming less than they already are. He tells us, *'Be for yourself what you want others to be for you. People will treat you as you treat yourself.'*

When you *live* the awareness of knowing that you have within you the knowledge that will set you free, you become a creative light of your own inner universe, and nothing will dim its radiance.

Not wanting to be, but being.
Not wanting to be seen, but seeing.
Not wanting the Light, but being the Light.

This is wisdom.

THE WORD

WE READ AND HEAR A LOT about the power of the word, 'In the beginning was the word', 'The word will set you free' or, 'The word came out of the fire' and so on. But exactly what does Thoth mean by *The Word*? Which word? And how are we supposed to use it?

In the Emerald Tablets, Thoth has given a long explanation on the power of one particular word. He tells us that the power of the word is in its sound. The word he uses is obviously meaningless. *"The Word"* he tells us is *"Zin-Uru"*. So how are we to pronounce it if the power is in the sound?

As in all his writings Thoth uses analogy, or he hides the message in partial explanations. This is sometimes due to translation difficulties between when the Tablets were moulded and the present day. The difficulty of translation has caused many strange and erroneous explanations of what Thoth is trying to teach. Only those with open minds and positive thoughts will search for the deeper meaning to see the truth in Thoth's teachings.

This particular translation tells us that when Thoth found the door to secret wisdom, he was able to open it because he knew *The Word*, but that the door to the secret mysteries would stay closed to everyone who didn't realise that it is the vibration that opens the door to natural and spiritual worlds. The vibrations of negative words and thoughts are not strong enough to open doors that reveal the Light, and words and thoughts which are destructive in their intention lock doors even more tightly shut than they were before you failed in opening them.

In what follows, Thoth is giving an example of how to unlock the doors to the natural world. It must not be taken literally but as an example of the power of sound. He begins by saying that he has not taken food or water before beginning this work, and that he had passed seven times and seven times through the fire. He continues that he used the drum of a serpent, and wearing a robe of purple and gold he put on his head a crown of silver, and around himself a circle of cinnabar. (It was a wise decision not to eat or drink while working with cinnabar, since it is a poison if ingested.)

Thoth tells us that he lit the circle of cinnabar, then using *The Word* and raising his arms above his head, he shouted out a command to the Lords of the Two Horizons, the watchers of the Treble Gates, to open the gates and release the one they keep imprisoned. Once he had opened the door he called to one of the daughters, who lives in this hidden world. One who was fairer than any human (so here Thoth is obviously implying that he is not communicating with mankind). He called to her, to leave the spaces of darkness and come into the world of men.

The Lords of Arulu parted to allow this fair maiden to come into the light. She was now free to live in the light of the sun, as a Child of Light.

Now let us look at what Thoth has done.

He has simply taken an example from nature to explain a spiritual law. First, he dresses himself in what can only be described as the appearance of an insect, and beating the drum would make a vibration similar to the buzzing sound of insects. With the crown on his head he indicates that he is calling for the highest member of the family, a king or queen.

He then puts a circle of cinnabar around himself, which in the distant past was said to induce a dream state, though it is also likely to induce a state of drowsiness in insects, especially when it is heated and produces smoke – hence, he lit the circle of cinnabar. He does not say the circle is on the floor, it is more likely to be around his waist in some sort of container. Cinnabar is also a pinkish hue, the colour of the energy of a high spiritual vibration.

What Thoth is doing is explaining how to move from one dimension to the next, by using bees as an example. Especially the queen, the fair maiden, as she leaves the darkness of the hive to come into the sunlight. He mentions the guardians of the Treble Gates. The guardians being the Masters who let you through from one plane to the next when you are ready. From this we understand that humans live in a dark place and are called into the light when the time is right.

The entrance to the hive, Arulu, is always guarded by bees to prevent any foreign bees or other intruders from entering and causing disharmony. He also calls the guardians the Lords of the Two Horizons. This is the time between dusk and dawn, when night gives way to day.

Once the smoking cinnabar has put the bees into a calm and drowsy state, Thoth uses the word *Zin-Uru* to entice the young queen bee out of the hive. In nature, the only vibration that would entice a young queen bee to leave the hive is a vibration she recognises as safe, which is the vibration in the sound the drones of the hive make when the queen is about to leave. The bees guarding the entrance to the hive would not allow a young queen to leave before the correct time had come, or before the suitable conditions were met.

The closest one can get to the sound and vibration of a buzzing bee is the word *Zin-Uru*. Let the word buzz through your lips to sound like a buzzing bee, short on the '*Zin*' and long on the '*Uruuuuu*'… I have pronounced this vibration in workshops with surprising results. Let the vibration buzz from your lips for as long as your breath will sustain it, and as it requires very little air when done correctly, the sound can be continued for a minute or more. Anyone within the range of the sound will be affected, if the vibration is right.

From this example it is easy to see the similarities between a young queen bee leaving the hive to begin a new life, and a soul leaving the Cycle of Life and Death to enter into a new stage in a higher world of awareness filled with Light. Thoth has, in his symbolic way, shown that the word itself is not important. It is the vibration the word or thought produces that is important. He waves his arms in the air as a bee would wave its antennae, it is the way insects communicate, vibration being the language of the natural world.

By playing the part of a bee, Thoth is demonstrating his point in a way that is not to be taken too seriously. The queen of the hive is one of several, and the one who has overcome the many struggles in her short life to reach the Light of Freedom. Other queens succumb to the difficulties and do not survive to leave the hive for the Light, and a new beginning. In spiritual terms it is the same for all life, everyone must struggle to reach the Light.

I do not know if he was deliberately trying to confuse or hide the secret of the power of sound. But if he was, he has certainly been very successful. After Thoth's records were discovered and translated, sometime in the 15th century, people began dressing up as magicians, putting pyramid-shaped hats on their heads and marking circles around themselves on the floor, waving their arms in the air, uttering bizarre words, banging drums and expecting such effects to induce some sort of underworld figure to appear. In some secret societies this sort of 'mumbo jumbo' is still practiced today.

There is one other thing to which we have not yet given any attention. At the beginning, he told us that he passed seven times seven through the fire. It is interesting to note that a young queen bee takes seven days from larva to pupa, before emerging as a queen and taking a following of bees with her when she leaves the hive. By stating the number, seven times seven, he suggests that forty-nine is the age a person can expect to have reached before being sufficiently experienced in life and ready to lead or have followers, whether you are male or female.

The whole idea of this elaborate and confusing explanation has been to explain to the uninitiated the secret of the word. That the secret is in the vibration or energy of the word. Using the right word will produce a vibration that will take the soul out of this dark physical world and into a higher awareness. Words such as love, children, or flowers all have a soft vibration, which are soothing and inviting. Other words such as, *'you must,'* or *'have to,'* as well as words spoken in anger or disagreement will produce a hard and attacking vibration, which attracts more of the same negative energy.

Thoughts produce vibrations in the same way and have to be in harmony with the energy and vibration of the plane you want to reach. You need to have the right thoughts before you can move to a higher plane.

It is what you think that is important, not what you do.

Now let us go back to the beginning, *'In the beginning was The Word.'*

Before words there are thoughts, and all thoughts produce their own unique energy which have their own unique vibration. Thoughts of contentment produce harmonious vibrations, while thoughts of anger produce destructive vibrations. If you enter a house where there has been an argument for example, you will feel it in the atmosphere. It will feel uncomfortable and you will not want to stay there for long.

In hospitals, if you are sensitive enough you can feel the energy of fear in the atmosphere. Whereas if you enter a home where there is peace and happiness you will feel uplifted and energised. Some thoughts attract, some thoughts hold you at bay. Thoughts of fear are intense and cold, but loving thoughts of children are soft and warm. What you think creates an energy that tells people, and particularly animals, what sort of person you are and what your intensions are.

The vibration, Thoth tells us, is what emerged at the beginning of time, from the chaos of unbalanced energies. It was seen as the flame at the beginning of all that is. The flame is a positive energy, rising from the disorder of negative energy, bringing order out of chaos. It was a positive vibration, heat, that rose out of the energy of chaos.

I am a healer, and to help people I put positive thoughts around the ones I am helping. Distance is no barrier to the effectiveness of thoughts, which is the whole basis of a prayer. Positive thoughts for wellbeing and health, to bring the one you are praying for back into physical or mental harmony. Thoughts of worry or anger on the other hand, especially fear or hate, will have the complete opposite effect, making any situation worse.

If you are sensitive to energy it is possible to feel the vibrations of a variety of different thoughts. Everyone has their own unique vibration, based on what they are thinking. Those who are more aware will sometimes see colours around people, something we refer to as the aura. This is no more than the vibration of thoughts being radiated in that moment.

There is a photographic technique known as Kirlian Photography, which produces an image of your thoughts, in colour, at the moment the photograph is taken, and shows that every thought-vibration has its own unique vibrational colour. Negative energy will always have a dull colour, and dominating thoughts will have a darker or stronger shade.

Happy thoughts are bright and clear. Fear, which radiates a cold grey colour, has an existence that is very real. It is a permanent background vibration in this dark world called Earth. If you are sensitive to vibrational energies you can feel the energy of fear all around. Negative people have no protection against this intrusive emotional energy of fear, since they are of a very similar vibration. Only positive thoughts distance you from the ill effects of such negative vibrations.

Apart from such fleeting thoughts there is also a deeper and more subtle vibration surrounding you, radiating an energy that has become a permanent feature of your personality. This is the vibration of your general attitude and the accumulation of thoughts over many lifetimes, which have become your underlying personality. This is who you really are, emotionally.

Every life is just one piece in a puzzle of a thousand pieces.

You become what you think and not what you say or do, which is often different to what you think. Your spiritual personality will radiate a bright clear light, but when the personality has become dominated by emotion, the radiating energy will be a variety of colours, depending on the thoughts dominating the soul's personality.

Thoth says he has shown us the keys to greater worlds. The thoughts we live from dawn till dusk will determine if we are able to use what he has taught and become Children of Light. There are no secrets in the world of thoughts, what we are thinking is what we become, and that can always be seen, even though we might not be heard.

Ask yourself, are your thoughts vibrating a positive, independent and creative energy? Or are they thoughts of dependency and selective in their preferences, and therefore negative and holding you indefinitely to the cycle of rebirth?

Good or bad, your every thought is a prayer, creating a vibrational image of who you are.

Throughout his teaching, Thoth is asking us to be one with the Light and to reject the Path of the Dark, by which he means negative thinking. Vibrations are attracted to similar vibrations, colours are attracted to similar colours, and emotions are attracted to similar emotions. *'Like attracts like.'*

Negative thoughts attract negative thoughts, and negative thoughts are not in harmony with the vibrations of the higher Worlds of Light. Thoth keeps telling us, *'If you want to be free of the Cycle of Rebirth, change your thinking to thoughts of integrity, and be one with the Light.'*

Be prepared to change the negative thoughts that you hold dear and which you think are necessary in your life, but which are preventing you moving away from the situation you are in. Negative thoughts hold you to what is negative, positive thoughts attract you to what is positive and beneficial for your health and wellbeing. Only positive creative thoughts will lift you free of the low vibrating emotional energies that hold you to this dark plane of sunken Atlantis.

Perhaps, it is necessary to point out that aggressive energy, which might seem to be positive, is spiritually a destructive energy that comes from uncontrolled emotion.

Thoth continues his treatise with the same message, over and over again. Telling us to realise that the way back to Paradise is determined by the thoughts we have. If we want to be free and move into a brighter future, we must change our ways from negative emotional thinking to positive awareness. This does not mean becoming religious, which contains many emotionally negative ideas. He means that we need to be prepared to move away from the people or situations which hold us to negative emotions.

Emotional negative energy will not allow your soul to grow, which can be the cause of many health and life problems. It is positive awareness based on integrity that makes for understanding, compassion and unconditional acceptance of all existing life. A positive existence that will lift you into the Light, which attracts more of the same.

SPIRALS

THOTH SPEAKS ENDLESSLY of moving to the Light. He has already explained some of the exercises he uses to leave his body and how to have an out-of-body experience during an incarnation. But as he explains: once your life has finished, the only way to move into a higher dimension and prevent an unnecessary rebirth is to become free of your negative emotions. Or at least, have them under control, especially those that you believe you cannot live without. Being positive is a good start.

He now goes deeper with his explanations and reasons. In his records Thoth talks about circles, and it seems that this one word has many meanings. He explains that everywhere he searches or goes he travels in circles: circles within circles, circles up, or circles down... It is obviously not his intention to declare that he is going in circles, which would mean that he is not getting anywhere. There is only one way we can understand most of these descriptions of circles and that is if we imagine them as spirals.

Thoth has already told us that energy does not move in straight lines but goes in circles, which I understand to be spirals. Not even light travels in straight lines but in curves. He tells us that energy lifts on a clockwise spiral and compresses on a counter-clockwise spiral. He does not suggest that moving up a spiral is going to be easy.

We are told we need to struggle against whatever emotion or negative circumstances might try to hold us back, because negative thoughts spiral down. In the same way that the Earth spins anti-clockwise causing gravity, negative emotions spiral in the same direction, to the left, to keep us earth-bound. We even say of someone whose condition is getting worse that *'they are on a downward spiral.'* And down is not the direction we want to go.

If we want to be free of the gravitational pull which holds the soul to the body, we need to imagine ourselves spiralling up, that is clockwise or to the right. Doing this moves us into faster and higher energies, we have more power and we say we feel *'...uplifted,'* or even *'...inspired.'* Think of a church spire reaching up to the sunlight, it's not unlike a pyramid in symbolism.

When we realise that Thoth intends us to see a circle as a spiral, it all begins to make sense. If we follow a spiral we move away from something, either vertically up or down. Thoth explains that one of the purposes of the pyramids is to demonstrate that when an energy is put into the base of a pyramid it will spiral up to the apex, where it will appear to be spiralling faster than it does at the base. As the energy spirals around and up inside the pyramid, its force intensifies. At the apex of the pyramid, the intensity of the energy is at its maximum. This is a way of increasing the force of any spiralling energy.

In the case of water for example, to spin the force from a wide base to a narrow point increases the pressure.

To move out of your body, spin clockwise and imagine that you are spinning as if inside a pyramid. It is possible to feel the intensity of the energy at the top of your head. Of course you do not need to spin physically, you do it with the energy you are. Though certain people, such as the Muslim Sufi culture, spin themselves in a dance frenzy to induce hypnotic and other forms of trance states.

Energy always spirals and blood is a good example. The blood is infused with energy through the heart. This is what gives blood its power, a phenomenon first recognised in 1920. Blood spirals through the arteries because of the energy that is spiralling through it. It is the spiralling energy in the blood that gives it the power to force its way through the many miles of arteries, veins and capillaries before returning back to the heart, to be reinforced with more energy. It is a fundamental fact of nature, which is often overlooked, that energy is a spiralling force. A spiralling thrust always has more force than a straight-line thrust.

Therefore, if you want to increase your energetic

powers, always imagine the energy spiralling through you and from you. If you are healing yourself or helping someone else, imagine energy spiralling through the area that needs improvement. It is much more effective than thinking of energy flowing or vibrating in a straight line. When you visualise an energy spiralling to your point of focus, you will achieve the purpose of your thoughts with more certainty and power.

Thoth explains that if you want to leave your body, improve your life, or stay healthy, you need to overcome all the negative attitudes and emotions, which will be working against you. You would not want a destructive negative energy flowing into your heart and through your body. Any thoughts that are out of harmony with happiness or contentment, such as arguments or doubts, are negative and destructive. Doubt in particular is a big negative force, which prevents or reverses an upwards spiralling movement.

A negative force will spiral down away from the point of interest, pulling energy with it. This is why negative attitudes are so self-defeating and will hold you to the slow vibrations of rebirth. It is also the reason why some therapists feel the illness and problems of their patients after a session. If the therapist has a negative energy, they will attract the negative energy of the patient into themselves, rather than reinforcing the patient with positive healing energy. Positive thoughts on the other hand spiral up, pulling energy in as they move forward, or as in meditation, taking the soul into the Light Levels to be enhanced with more positive energy.

All consciousness, all thoughts, are spirals of energy, either negative or positive, but they will always be moving. They can never be still: nature does not have a static or neutral state. The awareness of the natural world is spiralling on an upwards projection at the beginning of its life or season, and spiralling down at the end of its life or season. The life in a tree spirals up in the spring, and down in the late autumn. Not because of negativity though, but to stay in harmony with nature in its sleep.

At the end of life the soul spirals away from what has been holding it, and to where it spirals will depend on the thoughts it has become by the end of life. Only mankind with its emotions can reverse a natural positive flow and take itself into negative situations. Eventually all negative thoughts, intentional and unintentional, will deplete the person, plant or animal within the area of its negativity. You cannot forever hold back against the force of your own negativity, and eventually your physical and mental health will begin to break down. Learn to control your emotions as quickly as you can, because all negative thoughts will result in destruction, your own or those of others.

This is what the Dark Forces are constantly working to achieve. Fortunately, the dark energy of chaos is restricted to the Earth and lower Astral Levels, and people with negative energies will be unable to move into the higher levels of the Astral World, or the Light. You cannot spiral up with negative thoughts, as their direction is downwards. Remember what Thoth has told us, it is your lowest thoughts that determine your destiny and not your occasional higher or more positive ones. Not until you have become a Child of the Light, free of all negativity, will you reach the Realms of Light.

Circles within Circles

Thoth tells us that there are nine circles above and fourteen circles below. These two sets of numbers puzzled me, until I realised that their total of twenty-three is the number of chromosomes in every cell of the human body, and almost every other species on Earth.

DNA is the hereditary material in all forms of life, existing as a double helix – a spiral in a spiral or as it has been translated, a circle in a circle. There can be no mistaking that Thoth had an in-depth understanding of DNA, details of which have only become known to science in the last century. He goes on to say that the circles, or spirals, are units of consciousness, which work in harmony with the law. I believe Thoth is talking about the law of genetics. The two spirals, he tells us, will eventually come together to be made perfect.

Thoth talks about physical consciousness, which is different to spiritual awareness, and when read with an open mind one can see that consciousness, as he puts it, is a chromosome, or a set of chromosomes.

Every consciousness follows its own path and the more we use our mind, the more information the chromosomes will hold, which allows them to evolve to be more than they were. Thoth tells us that all life, including plant and animal life, is striving to improve, building greater laws into its spirals.

He continues that knowledge is gained by experience and that new spirals of consciousness are created from new knowledge. Simultaneously, positive thoughts advance the soul with increased spirals of awareness. This whole piece is telling us about the evolution of life on the planet Earth, and the advancement of the soul into higher levels of awareness at the same time. It is not only about the evolution of the physical, but also about the evolution of the soul.

Thoth says that the fourteen chromosomes at the base evolve differently to the other nine above. The fourteen are responsible for the stability of the physical, while the other nine are responsible for the potential of the soul. These nine chromosomes are connected to spiritual awareness and therefore not as easily defined as the other fourteen. Emotions, being part of the education of the soul, also find their place in the chromosomes. Once they are under control, the physical and spiritual can work together without the interference of negativity – for a happier, healthier and longer experience.

It is incredible that Thoth was referring to DNA and aware of the different functions between the chromosomes at least as early as the beginning of the Egyptian civilisation. He is explaining the Law of Evolution and how all life evolves perhaps hundreds of thousands of years before Darwin's work on evolution. Thoth says that any life that does not appear to have the developed awareness of mankind is no less complete at its present stage, and that everything in nature has awareness. There is DNA in everything, some of it still undeveloped and some of it developed beyond the level of human awareness. In the final analysis all life is equal, developing through the combined consciousness of experience.

All life is connected through DNA and the Chakra System. Though we are evolving on a soul level, both physical consciousness and spiritual awareness rely on the past experiences of nature. We evolve from the Halls of Amenti with all the information that nature has preserved since the beginning of time. No life, no level of awareness, should ever be considered to be less than any other. We are all connected and interdependent. Without the combined forces of all lives, in all of nature, nothing would evolve.

Any feelings of superiority, which act to separate the individual from the totality of nature's awareness, will delay the individual's development. Our DNA has been derived from nature and as Thoth keeps telling us, it is in nature that all secrets are found. There will always be awareness greater than our own and if we are to continue to evolve, we need to acknowledge the contribution of life from every level, including mineral, vegetable, and animal, in the makings of an individual.

This advice from Thoth enforces his reasoning that negative thinking is destructive in many ways. It not only delays the evolution of our physical lives but delays the evolution of the soul, and if we do anything to obstruct another person's expression of themselves, we also obstruct their development, delaying the time when both will move into the Light. Negative and destructive emotions delay not only the individual's evolution, but also the lives of those who inherit the negatively poled DNA.

What is normally considered materially important to life, is of no importance to anyone who is concerned with improving their own evolving soul. It is what you think that is of the highest importance, as you become what you think and not what other people think of you. As mentioned before, *'We were not born to be a slave to the expectations of others,'* but the moment you begin to be concerned about what other people think about you, you have become their slave.

The soul will evolve to be what you are thinking: positive, selfless, generous and filled with creative thoughts, to become more than you were, or: negative, selfish, destructive and full of doubting thoughts, which block any improvement in your own life and that of succeeding generations, both spiritually and physically.

Thoth continues to emphasise the importance of the spirals and the necessity of the spirals in the double helix staying in harmony. Harmony, which comes from a positive and balanced mind. It is when harmony between the two spirals is lost that health, mental and physical, begins to break down. If we are going to live a healthy and happy life beyond one hundred years, without showing signs of aging, our thinking has to remain balanced, which means being content and satisfied with what we have and what we are doing. The poles, the electromagnetic forces in the body, must continue in harmony, one with the other.

Perfect health requires perfect balance between these two forces. Thoth is telling us that a long and healthy life is dependent on this balance, and balance is measured by contentment. No one can prescribe a pill of contentment, there is nothing from outside our own awareness that can give us the sensation of contentment. Contentment is something we cause for ourselves, in accepting what we have and who we are, knowing we can and will become more.

When we feel unhappy, the electromagnetic balance of the body changes, and this is when physical and mental problems begin to creep in. Sometimes our situation and needs change and we are no longer content with life. It is when we lose our contentment that we begin to become negative. So, how can we regain the contentment we have lost?

It is all about how we judge the situation we are in. Do not let emotion dominate the way you think. If you let anger and frustration control or determine your attitude, you increase the electric side of your nature and then the body begins to overheat. This is when you make mistakes, annoy people, and generally overreact. If you should become worried or fearful, you increase the negative side of the poles and begin to feel cold, lose the drive to do anything, become depressed and lethargic, and dependent on others.

Neither of these reactions are good for your health and happiness. You need to stay unemotional about your situation, and consciously choose how you are going to react. You can choose to feel happy or sad, angry or calm. There are a multitude of emotions you can choose from, but whatever your reaction, it has been your choice. No one can make you sad, angry or happy, you choose your emotions, no one can cause you to have a particular reaction. This is free will. Either you or your emotions will decide your reaction to any particular situation. If you are unable to choose, then you are no longer in charge and your emotions are already controlling you. You have become a slave to your own emotions.

If you are not in a good situation for some reason, recognise it and then, without getting excited or worried, decide what the best way forward is and how you are going to manage it. As far as it is humanly possible, stay emotionally detached. Do not let your emotions take over your life, and do not let the attitudes of others infect you. The moment this happens you have become a slave to your emotional self and those around you, which will cause all sorts of problems. So, if you have any problems with your health or wellbeing, it is time to ask yourself, *'Is an emotion the cause of my problem?'*

If it is, do something about the emotion before embarking on a course of medical treatment. This is such a small question, but the answer will have enormous consequences for your health and happiness. If you are being emotional about a situation you will either be overreacting or being negative. Either way is going to have an effect on your health and wellbeing, as you will be putting your electromagnetic poles out of balance.

If you feel the negative side of your balance is too strong, then do something physical like going for a long walk or to the gym, to stimulate the body's positive energy. When you start to feel agitated about something, go into the garden and relax, or involve some other calming activity such as meditating, to bring yourself back into balance. Then you will be able to make unemotional decisions about your situation, decisions which come from your soul and which will be right for your situation, without any future side-effects.

It is important to remember that the attitudes of other

people can influence your own electrical balance. Knowing this helps to stay in your own balance and block the emotional imbalance of other people and their situations, which could otherwise have a negative effect on your own health.

There are many life situations which cause people to become emotional and remove the responsibility for reasoned judgement from the soul. But the one situation which I believe affects many of us are the radio waves that are swamping the Earth. It is my personal conclusion that an excess of electric forcefields, which the modern world relies on for communication and entertainment, is leading to physical problems and mental instability. Together with uncontrolled negative emotions, they will eventually cause a worldwide breakdown in society.

It was shown many years ago that living close to high-voltage power lines was often the cause of depression and other negative states of mind. I know from my own experiments that the opposite, low-frequency sound waves, stimulate the senses. Some music overstimulates the mind so that it results in aggressive behaviour, stimulating the electric side of our balance.

I was once involved in a double-blind trial at a British University, where 100 chicken eggs were placed in water which had sound waves passed through it. Another 100 eggs were placed in untreated water for the same amount of time of 40 minutes. When the eggs hatched, the number and type of mutations in the chickens which had been in the water with sound waves passing through, was horrendous. In contrast, there were no abnormalities in the control group. It was explained that sound waves have a physical effect because they disrupt the electromagnetic balance of the body.

Thoth, writing several thousand years ago, mentions flying machinery, space travel, world wars, and other phenomena that was unthought-of two hundred years ago. He also prophesised that the emotionally negative influence of life will become so unbalanced that civilization will destroy itself, and humanity will be reduced to the original barbaric state in which he found it.

He goes on to state that humanity will rise again out of the dust to ascend to greatness, but next time, humanity will have learned how to stay emotionally positive, and the souls who have made this jump in evolution will continue their journey to the Light. They will have learned how to leave their bodies when it suits them, and not be forced to do so at an inconvenient time.

As Thoth warns, there will always be a struggle between the forces of Light and Dark; it is not a natural state for the electromagnetic forces to be separated. The soul, which is positive in awareness and imagination, is the Light. The Dark and negative energy is what is seen around all life that has not yet reached an independent soul level. The soul controls its destiny by its own thoughts. Emotion interferes with the balance if not prevented. Negative energy is always trying to return to its original state of chaos. Positive energy becomes stronger over time, and many lives. It was the power of the positive side that brought calm out of chaos.

Thoth asks that you look at your life and to ask yourself as an emotional being, 'Are you doing what you can to be more positive and help others, or are you being critical and an obstacle in your own life and that of others?

'Are you empowering the law of positive influence to overcome all forms of destruction, or are you a negative influence encouraging disruption in the peace and calm of yourself and others?'

To plan your destiny, control what you think.

Thoth ends this section of the Emerald Tablets telling us that there is nothing more important than aiming for the perfection of the soul. Do not be negative and part of chaos, which is everywhere around you. Look inside yourself and decide, what and who you want to be.

Only when you are free of emotion or in control of it, will you be able to change, to attract or reject the many situations in your life, with the power of your unemotional positive thoughts.

THE DOCTRINE

THOTH KNEW THE TIME was coming when he would have to leave Planet Earth for a few centuries. His concern was how would mankind, to whom he had given his knowledge, hold the information together and teach the knowledge and wisdom he had given, without putting their own thoughts into it? How could he help future generations remember the way to regain entry to the Lost World of Atlantis?

He had selected the more imaginative of the people around him to create the great civilization of Egypt, and it was to them he gave the foundation of a story that would keep people away from chaotic attitudes and selfish ways of living. He instructed the teachers that they must not corrupt what he had taught, and to ensure that his teachings would continue unchanged they must make a doctrine of them, with rituals and rules that would fix the laws in the minds of men. However, it was not a religion as we understand it today. It would be true to say it was a philosophy on the way to live and stay in harmony with nature and the Great Lord, from whom everything is created. Thoth advocated the absolute belief in a single deity, who could appear in many different forms and could be seen in everything.

Thoth, creator of written language, was total in his belief that all knowledge is represented in nature. Therefore, it was natural that he should use the World of Nature to illustrate his thoughts, and use animals to represent the laws of creation. To transfer words into written symbols was unique at the time, when Thoth was raising humanity from its barbaric state to one of civilisation. Hieroglyphs were no more than a system of specialised, organised cave drawings which simple people, not knowing any written language, would be able to understand. It is a total misunderstanding to believe that the Egyptians worshiped many Gods, because they used animals to represent written language.

As Thoth teaches, God is omnipresent and therefore everywhere and in everything at the same time, but still a single deity. Using nature to represent what is being taught is a strong way of imprinting the ideas onto the mind, and an easy way to remember the laws of creation. For example, the baboon was used to represent the judges of law (amongst other things), because they cry when the sun goes down and darkness takes over, and sing when the light returns.

Apart from using nature as an analogy in forms of animals, birds, fish and insects to tell the story of creation, Thoth also used the act of sacrifice to teach people that it was good to give in return of receiving. But sacrifice did not include blood or slaughter, nature and life were too important and sacred to be destroyed. Sacrifice was meant to be caring for nature, giving something back of your own efforts to balance the constant taking from it.

In the doctrine that his Egyptian teachers would share with the people, Thoth gives a list of names, symbols and rituals to represent the Truth. He has already shown that life is a battle between the Dark, "*Duat*" the House of Illusion, and the Light, "*Sekhet Hepspet*" the House of the Gods (as in Spirits of Light).

Thoth built a story around the way to live a positive life and the consequences if you do not follow the laws of nature. Having created the Egyptian doctrine with rules, rituals and ceremony, he insisted that it be followed without additions or admissions until his return.

Thoth further introduced the belief and understanding of reincarnation in his doctrine. There is a famous manuscript, inscribed many thousands of years ago at the time of the Pharaoh Seti I which reads:

Men do not live once to vanish forever, but live several lives, in different places.

God has many faces, but it is always the same God who no one knows.

The fact that Egypt became one of the most powerful and civilised cultures in the then-known world, and lasted for many thousands of years, is proof of how successful Thoth's teaching became. Unsurprisingly, after thousands of years of telling and retelling, the original message in the story became lost or misinterpreted and new religions born from it have tried to improve on the old beliefs. In doing so, they have in many aspects lost the meaning of life and death as a means of regaining their rightful inheritance to a life in Atlantis, or as we call it, *Paradise*.

Thoth now wants the original truth retold. He tells us that there are no mysteries: *'Mystery is knowledge you don't have, and there is nothing mysterious about the Keys of Life. It is all based on positive, creative imagination and rising above negativity.'*

He tells us that once man has conquered all obstacles and overcome the Dark and is able to enter the Light, the world and its secrets will be open to him. Nothing will be hidden, and he will learn the greater secrets of moving through time, to see back as well as forth. He will learn the secrets of space and be able to be in any place at any time, with the will of his own awareness and imagination. But if he prefers the Dark energies, it would be better to fall into the Fire of Chaos to emerge and begin again, rather than suffer the eternal Darkness of Unknowing.

The mysteries of life are hidden, and only those who are sincere in reaching the Light will find the hidden portals that lead out of the Earth Force and into the

Light. Thoth tells us that in his writings are the keys, some hidden in symbols, that will unlock the mysteries which will show the Pathway to Light. There are those who will always deny the Truth, but those who seek it will find it.

He says that the initiated will understand what he has to say about the Secrets of Three, but that the profane will completely misunderstand or ignore these mysteries.

'So listen and consider what I say, and then the Light will come to you.'

Three are the qualities of the Lord.
Infinite Awareness, Infinite Wisdom, Infinite Power.

Nothing can exist without the Three.
They are the Source of Creation.
Awareness, Imagination, Wisdom.

Three come out of the balance of the Three.
All Life, all Good, all Power.

Three powers that make a Master.
Transmuting evil, assisting good, using judgement.

Three are the powers available from the Lord.
Divine Awareness, possessing perfect knowledge.
Divine Wisdom, knowing all possible means.
Divine Imagination, from which all things are created.

There are Three States of Existence.

The State of Nature, where all things have their beginnings.

The State of Awareness, where all things evolve.

The State of Chaos, where all things end or are lost.

Three Necessities to control all things.
Division of chaos into Dark and Light.
Separation of positive and negative.
Wisdom of knowing the difference.
Three Paths of the Soul.
The physical, through emotion, into Light.

There are Three Obstacles of the Soul.
Lack of endeavour to obtain knowledge.
Detachment from the Lord and creativity.
Attachment to evil.

There are Three obstacles in man.
Doubt, Desire, and Superiority.

Thoth's great concern remains that the negative forces flowing through the energies of the Earth are again becoming stronger than the positive forces, which keep the universe in balance. At the same time, a wave of pure creative energy is descending from the summit of the Atlantean Continent, to create a new spiritual plane. When the force of this energy reaches the most distant parts of the continent, the lowest plane will be forced even further away.

At that point the Earth will tip on its axis and the waters will wash over its surface once more, and human life will be lost. The Earth will become one with the Dark Worlds, but those who have made the evolutionary jump will rise again, on the newly created plane. And this time, they will be free of the Dark that has brought so much chaos and destruction.

Thoth's warning at this point is to those who struggle to be one with the Light. They should strive against the forces who deny the Truth, and keep on the path that leads to the Light. Let go of everything that holds you to the Earth, especially fear, desire and superiority. Look beyond your securities in life, turn to the Light and feel its pull, which is attracting you to itself. Soon the Dark will descend across the Earth, like infinite night. But if you trust in the Light and find it within you, it will lift you away from the Dark when the waves come crushing down.

THE BEGINNING

THOTH CONTINUED HIS QUEST to find the source of all things. Wherever he went, whatever he found or saw, everything was the same, every space was just a copy of another space. He tells us that he found worlds within worlds: he had found the secret of space in holograms. Thoth saw that deep in the essence of matter there are many secrets, but all secrets are held in the first secret, and the same laws applied wherever he went.

Thoth realised that only the original Light can recreate itself and change, and that everything else is just a copy. He saw that there are nine planes, connected one to the other but kept separate by spirals of energy. He saw that a plane is a spiralling energy with a faster or slower vibration than the plane above or below.

He learned from the Nine Lords, who were responsible for the continued balance of space, that as humanity ascends from one plane to the next, it has to adjust its consciousness to be in harmony with the plane it is moving into. Thoth learned that it was the level of one's own positive and creative thinking that is the main factor in the ascension through the planes.

He saw that through all space flowed different forms

of life, which are unknown to each other. He realised that it was *time* within the spirals which held one space separate from another. That space is divided by time, and that it is in time that consciousness exists. He knew that mankind did not originate as a physical being, but became physical in its quest for independence, which is the evolution of the soul from the lowest of all states, which is Dark, to the highest, which is Light.

Thoth asked the Great Lord to help him find the secret of time and space. The answer was that he would only know these secrets when he was free of time and space, since he had to be outside an energy if he wanted to see into it. The soul is only free of time and space when it has lost its dependency on the energy of others and has become totally independent and free of a need for an emotional personality.

It is the soul's awareness that creates its own world, using the energy of its imagination. Everything must first enter the imagination before it can be created and if nothing is done with the image, it will continue to exist as a thought-form, as a hologram, such as it does in a dream. If the soul requires the image to permanently materialise, it will need to have learned the secrets and laws of creation and find the source of his or her own awareness.

You will need to know *everything* about yourself before you are able to manifest life outside yourself. The keys to the secrets, the potential of life, can only be found within one's self. Mankind is the key to its own secrets.

**To be more than you are,
first know all that you are.
What you seek is already within you.**

The soul is the gateway to all the secrets of life and only the soul is free of space and time, to have an awareness that is really free. Identity is held by a need to know itself through others. This, it was explained, meant that dependency was a need to see ourselves through the thoughts and eyes of others.

Dependency has never increased awareness. To have knowledge and wisdom you need to look inside your soul; it is there that you will find the pathway which leads to the ethereal libraries of Atlantis, where all knowledge is stored. Search for the Flame of Life within yourself, and do not waste energy on the negative dependency of others. In ascending, you reconnect with the highest, but this can only be achieved through your own independent efforts.

Thoth was taken back to the beginning of time, where he saw that everything was chaos. There were no laws and there was no order. There was just a confusion of energy. Then Thoth looked deeper and saw a glimmer of Light in the darkness of chaos. It was like a little flame, struggling to break free of the Dark.

Then the voice of the Great Lord said to Thoth, *'Hear*

and understand. This Little Flame is the source of all things. It is order, growing out of chaos. It was a thought, an awareness, with a need to create itself without fear, desire, or superiority. Alone it brought itself out of chaos and from this little flame, everything has grown.

'In the beginning was the Word, but before the Word was given, there had to be the Thought. It was the Thought that gives birth to the Word, and the Word was a vibration that spread in spirals, so that it could not be caught. This Little Flame became all things created, because only positive energy is creative.

'The spoken thought was so great that all things that are, were created from it. Everything that is came into awareness because of the creative imagination in that Little Flame. The Little Flame grew with power to push the Darkness of Chaos away from itself. This Little Flame encouraged more like itself to evolve out of the chaos. But the Dark of the Chaos continues to exist, trying to reverse the Light and prevent more Light from being born. All Light, all souls, are surrounded by the Darkness of Chaos and must ever be strong to resist the call to return to the Dark and become lost.'

'This,' said the Great Lord, *'is the source of all, the wisdom for which you have been searching.'*

'Tell me about Time and Space,' Thoth inquired.

'Man is the reason for time and space. Listen carefully to my words and dwell on their meaning.

'Space is the growing awareness in which thoughts exist. So, there can be no such thing as empty space. Thoughts and space are synonymous.

'Time is the distance of awareness, as it moves from thought to thought. Time is every thought and the distance between every thought. Therefore, there is no time without space and there is no space without time, and so the two exist one within the other. This is the double helix of all awareness.

'Every thought is the birth of an opening in space, causing more time.'

Thoth watched the Little Flame as it shone with the essence of awareness. He became one with its power and realised that life is nothing but order, brought out of chaos, and that mankind is one with this Little Flame, which is the culmination of all the positive thoughts ever created.

Mankind, he realised, is just a little flame fighting back the Dark of Chaos. While Thoth was contemplating, the voice of the Great Lord came back into his thoughts.

'Know Thoth, that life is nothing but the Word, brought forth from the Fire.

'Look for the Path to the Light in the Flame and all its powers shall surely be yours. With positive awareness your soul was born out of chaos, but you must always be aware that the Dark is waiting to pull you back to itself.

'Through order you will find your way, you saw that the Light was born out of the Darkness. You saw that positive thoughts were the Light of the Flame. So, watch in your life to change disorder back into order and bring balance back into your soul. Quell all the chaos of emotion and you will have power and order in your life.

'Order, brought out of chaos, will bring the support of the source and give you the power of the spirals, to make your soul a Force with the Light. It will keep you free and extend you through the ages, so you continue to grow with the source of all. You will become a perfected child of the source, a Child of the Light.'

Thoth assures us that these words went deep into his heart and that he has ever since looked to keep his thoughts free from the disorder of negativity and the destruction it brings. Thoth had been shown that negativity is always the enemy of order and awareness. That negative thoughts weaken the life-force of the Light and bring nothing but Darkness and destruction to the Light in men.

He had been shown that everything created comes from the thoughts and imagination of the original Flame of Life. No-thing can come into existence without first being the energy of a thought. The thought then takes the shape and form of what was imagined.

Every grain of sand began life as a thought-form in the awareness of light, the light in that Little Flame.

Imaginative thoughts create energy in space, and the energy in every thought takes the shape of the thought.

The Great Lord returned to Thoth after he had pondered long and hard on the mysteries of life.

'Hear this Thoth,' he continued. *'Every creative thought is born from the energy of the Light. Everything that was ever created is held together with the light of the original thought.*

'Light is what holds the planes together.

'Light is what holds together all that exists.

'Light is the positive force of a creative imagination.

'No-thing was ever created with negative thoughts, and all negative thoughts will weaken the structure of your life, all life, and the time and space you live through.

'The Dark will always be seeking to return order back into chaos, through negative thoughts. And working through emotion, the Dark will destroy what the Light has created.

'Always look to the Light, keep your thoughts free of all but the oneness with every other light, for even emotional love will weaken the fabric of life.

'I have now shown you the mysteries of life, and the Flame that burns in your heart is the one you must keep burning bright. Stay free of the Dark because without Light, no-thing exists.'

This is when Thoth concludes all the wisdom he has gathered and lists the many laws humanity must follow, if they were to return to the Light of Atlantis. Egyptians of the past believed that these laws were from Thoth, originated many thousands of years ago, and came from a place called Atlantis.

From these many laws, and over an incredibly long period of time, have come the Ten Commandments of Moses. But, Moses changed those few laws from the personal of *'I will not'*, to the impersonal of *'You must not.'*

This has caused people to lose responsibility for themselves and expect others to change instead, when the only way to the Light is through personal responsibility.

As Thoth says, *'Give them my wisdom and let people ask questions of themselves, not of others. No man can be saviour to the soul of another, he comes to the Light with only his own soul.'*

You now have Thoth's wisdom as he learned it in Atlantis. He has given time and space to bring mankind from the barbaric beginning in which he found them to a place where they are able to seek their own way to knowledge. And from it, to gain the wisdom which is the Key to the Doors of Atlantis. Paradise, which is humanity's rightful inheritance.

Thoth waits to greet all who successfully complete the Pathway to the Light.

Printed in Great Britain
by Amazon